MY IDEA OF
EDUCATION

Swami Vivekananda

Compiled by
Dr. Kiran Walia

Aðvaita Ashrama

PUBLICATION DEPARTMENT
5 DEHI ENTALLY ROAD · KOLKATA 700 014

Published by
Swami Bodhasarananda
Adhyaksha, Advaita Ashrama
Mayavati, Champawat, Uttarakhand, Himalayas
from its Publication Department, Kolkata
Email : mail@advaitaashrama.org
Website : www.advaitaashrama.org

© *All Rights Reserved*
First Edition, July 2008
Seventh Reprint, September 2013
6M6C

ISBN 978-81-7505-305-2

Printed in India at
Trio Process
Kolkata 700 014

CONTENTS

PUBLISHER'S NOTE

Indian youths are now at the crossroads. On one side they see the pompous show of wealth, luxury, enjoyments, and on the other side they see millions of people without enough food or clothing, struggling to survive in miserable conditions. India's priceless spiritual heritage, which enshrines the eternal spiritual truths and wisdom discovered by the ancient Rishis, is now facing the challenge of materialistic values, and unethical modern trends reaching the youths via the internet, TV shows and mass media. Owing to competition, consumerism, etc. life has become stressful and aimless for present-day youngsters.

In this dire situation the life and teachings of Swami Vivekananda can be of immense benefit and help to all people. The teaching of Swami Vivekananda contains the distilled essence of India's spiritual treasures explained in the simplest language in the light of modern rational thought and science. They are universal in their scope and are meant for all people belonging to all strata of society, all religions and all races. Swamiji's powerful exhortations awaken the minds of youths, instil self-confidence and courage in them to face the problems of life, fill their hearts with love and spirit of service, goad them to tread always the moral path, and guide them through the difficulties and uncertainties of life.

The present book is a collection of some of the well-known teachings and exhortations of Swami Vivekananda, compiled from the 9-volume *Complete Works of Swami Vivekananda*. Thousands of copies of this book have already been sold. As a part of the celebration of Swamiji's 150th Birth Anniversary (2013-2014), this book is being made available at a subsidized price.

To give the readers at the outset a synoptic view of the Swami's thoughts and the Swami himself, we have included two additional write-ups. The first is a monograph by Swami Prabhananda, the present General Secretary and a senior monk of the Ramakrishna Order. Written at UNESCO's behest, it focuses on Swami Vivekananda's contribution to educational ideas. It was published in UNESCO's Prospects (Volume XXXIII, Number 2, June 2003) and is reproduced here with the permission of the author. The second article is by Swami Yatiswarananda (1889–1966), who was a Vice-president of the Ramakrishna Math and Ramakrishna Mission.

We are thankful to Prof. J. S. Rajput for writing a valuable Preface to this book and the interest he showed in this project. We hope that the book will serve as a handbook for students, teachers, parents, and all educationists, and inspire them to imbibe, and also impart, true education.

Belur Math
1 May 2011

PUBLISHER

PREFACE

One rarely comes across divinely enlightened and blessed individuals who precisely perceive and present a prophetic picture of the future. They are capable of envisioning the past, the present, and the future in continuity. Their ideas survive the boundaries of time and space. Swami Vivekananda was one such gift of God to humanity. He dedicated himself to the welfare of the entire humanity, and also spread the message of the essential unity of all faiths and religions, and the need for spiritual pursuits for achieving higher goals of human life.

Swami Vivekananda presented the true India to the whole world. The concept of *Vasudhaiva Kutumbakam*—the world is one family—is the only beacon light for survival, growth, and real progress for human society, particularly in the strife-torn world of today. It was perceived in India in ancient times by our learned sages and saints and has an eternal validity. Swami Vivekananda explained and elaborated it in the global context. What a superhuman articulation and presentation he bestowed on all of us! The whole world was mesmerized and began to look towards India, to explore and learn about its past glory. The basic tenets of the Indian tradition of creation, generation and dissemination of knowledge were expanded in tune with the requirements and needs of the times. At the present juncture of history, when the concept of a global village is being discussed all around, there is a greater need to acquire a subtle understanding of the thoughts of Swami Vivekananda on learning to live together and on universal brotherhood. Widespread awareness of his thoughts and ideas amongst teachers and would-be teachers is particularly important as they have the responsibility of educating the young.

Swami Vivekananda's ideas on various aspects of education are more relevant and are needed more today than probably during his own life time. Only he had the vision and the courage to articulate: "The true education, however, is not yet conceived of amongst us." Every time I recall this statement to myself or repeat it to an audience of teachers and teacher educators, I find it more and more motivating, evolving, and expanding. It exhorts everyone to strive hard, explore, discover, interpret and utilize all their talents for the benefit of young learners. His ideas elevate everyone who reads and understands the meaning and the imperatives. They are capable of transforming the perception of teachers. Imagine the shape of education once every teacher starts adoring the inherent divinity of each child in the temples of learning.

Over the last decade, I have vehemently pleaded the need for enhanced emphasis on value inculcation, nurturance, and development. Further, education must impart the awareness and knowledge of the basics of all the religions of the people of India. Religions are not the only source of values, but they are a major source of values. This alone is the positive and correct interpretation of secularism in the multireligious society that India is. Let me quote Swami Vivekananda: "If you attempt to get the secular knowledge without religion, I tell you plainly, vain is your attempt in India; it will never have a hold on the people".

On umpteen occasions, I found answers in the works of Swami Vivekananda to my own queries and concerns on various aspects of education. It gradually became uppermost in my mind that every teacher needs to be aware of the thoughts of

Swami Vivekananda on education. I suggested to my colleague Dr. Kiran Walia to procure a personal copy of the collected works of Swami Vivekananda along with other relevant and useful writings of others on him and about him. The idea was to prepare a concise yet comprehensive publication mainly for the use of teachers and teacher educators. It took some time. Several eminent scholars have given valuable suggestions which have definitely enhanced the quality of the contents. The late Swami Gokulanandaji, the then Head of the Ramakrishna Mission Centre in Delhi, suggested that the manuscript be sent to Swami Suhitanandaji, presently Assistant Secretary of the Ramakrishna Math and Ramakrishna Mission at the Headquarters at Belur Math in West Bengal, and the latter gave several valuable suggestions during the editing stage. We believe that the inclusion of the contributions of Swami Yatiswaranandaji and Swami Prabhanandaji at the beginning will be of great help to the readers in comprehending the essence of the thoughts of Swami Vivekananda. It gives me a sense of satisfaction that my suggestion has taken shape. I express my gratitude to all concerned. It is my fond hope that the teaching community will not only peruse through this book, but also study and teach it sincerely to their students for the benefit of the youth of India, on whom Swami Vivekananda pinned his great hopes for the rejuvenation and re-building of a glorious India. We may recall his prophetic utterance in this context: "Let us all work hard, my brethren; this is no time for sleep. On our work depends the coming of the India of the future. She is there, ready, waiting. She is only sleeping. Arise and awake and see her seated on her eternal throne, rejuvenated, more glorious than she ever was—this motherland of ours."

Professor J.S. Rajput
Chairperson, National Council of Teacher
Education (NCTE) (1994-1999) & Director, National Council of
Educational Research and Training (NCERT) (1999-2004)

SWAMI VIVEKANANDA
THE EDUCATIONIST PAR EXCELLENCE

Swami Vivekananda—His Life and Personality

A regal, majestic figure of commanding presence, vast learning and deep insight, Swami Vivekananda was barely 30 years old when he created a stir at the World's Parliament of Religions in Chicago in 1893. Three and a half years later, when he returned to India, his homeland, he was as a colossus of strength, courage, confidence, love, and manliness—the embodiment of the ideal of the 'man-making and character-building' education he propagated.

Swami Vivekananda was born Narendranath Datta on 12 January 1863 in Kolkata, in a respectable middle-class family. His father, Vishwanath Datta, was an attorney, and a lover of arts and literature. Although liberal-minded, Vishwanath was skeptical about religious practices. On the other hand, Narendra's mother, Bhuvaneshwari Devi, was a pious, kind-hearted lady, devoted to the Hindu traditions. The influence of each of his parents on Narendra was different, yet together they provided a congenial atmosphere for the precocious boy to grow into an energetic young man with high ideals.

During his formative years, he developed extraordinary mental abilities which some people either misunderstood or ignored, but which others appreciated and recognized as signs of an outstanding individual. As a child he liked to play at meditation and would easily become engrossed. Once when he was seated thus in meditation along with some of his friends, the sudden appearance of a cobra slithering across the floor drove all the children out of the room except Narendra, who remained absorbed in meditation.

Narendra's power of concentration—of fixing his mind on one thing while detaching it from everything else—was remarkable. In his later life he once shot in succession, twelve eggshells bobbing up and down on the water of a river, although he had never fired a gun before! No less striking was his self-control. He remained calm and unruffled, no matter how dramatic the situation he was in.

Ever since childhood, Narendra had great admiration for wandering monks, and he liked to think that one day he himself would become a monk. But his ambition only became evident during his college days at the Scottish Church College. He began to search out scholars and spiritual leaders in order to question them. But none of them could satisfy him. It was from Prof. William Hastie, principal of his college that he heard for the first time of Sri Ramakrishna, the saint of Dakshineswar. His meeting with Sri Ramakrishna in November 1881 proved to be a turning point in his life. About this meeting, Narendranath said:

> He [Sri Ramakrishna] looked just like an ordinary man, with nothing remarkable about him. He used the most simple language and I thought, 'Can this man be a great teacher?'—I crept near to him and asked him the question which I had been asking others all my life: 'Do you believe in God, Sir?' 'Yes,' he replied. 'Can you prove it, Sir?' 'Yes.' 'How?' 'Because I see Him just as I see you here, only in a much intenser sense.' That impressed me at once. ... I began to go to that man, day after day, and I actually saw that religion could be given. One touch, one glance, can change a whole life.[1]

Sri Ramakrishna's life was one of spiritual experience and achievement. He also discovered some truths of great significance to all of us today. About this Sri Ramakrishna said:

I have practiced all religions—Hinduism, Islam, Christianity—and I have also followed the paths of the different Hindu sects. I have found that it is the same God towards whom all are directing their steps, though along different paths.[2]

Sri Ramakrishna carefully guided Narendra and a band of other young dedicated disciples, and the Master chose Narendra as the leader of the group. After the Master's passing away, these young devotees gathered together in a dilapidated house in Baranagore, a northern suburb of Kolkata, which became the first centre of the Ramakrishna Order. With a total rejection of material possessions and an unshakable commitment to their Master and his teachings, they endured unbelievable privations and devoted themselves to spiritual practices.

Travelling throughout the length and breadth of India, mostly on foot, Narendra was trying to work out a purpose for his life. While on the road, he often faced starvation and frequently found himself with nowhere to stay. To Narendra, this was an opportunity to study India and its needs at first hand. He observed that his country possessed a priceless spiritual heritage, but had failed to reap its benefit. The weak points were poverty, caste, neglect of the masses, oppression of women and a faulty system of education. How was India to be regenerated? He came to the conclusion:

We have to give back to the nation its lost individuality and raise the masses. ... Again, the force to raise them must come from inside.[3]

Narendranath Datta had by this time been transformed into Swami Vivekananda, and he had found his life's mission. Taking a broad look at the early part of his life we can see that there were four influences that formed his personality and philosophy:

1. India was then under British rule and was experiencing an upheaval in its cultural life. British rule had brought India into the world community, and English education and modernization had brought new hope. Yet, reflecting on the actual result of all this, Vivekananda said, 'A few hundred, modernised, half-educated, and denationalised men are all that there is to show of modern English India—nothing else.'[4] In his youth, Narendra 'became fascinated with the Evolutionism of Herbert Spencer,' and 'translated Spencer's book on 'Education' into Bengali for Gurudas Chattopadhyaya, his publisher.'[5] It is also said that Narendra exchanged correspondence with Herbert Spencer for some time.[6] But, alongside his study of Spencer and other Western philosophers, he also delved deep into Indian Sanskrit scriptures.

2. Sri Ramakrishna, the saint of Dakshineswar, had a profound influence on his contemporaries who were considered the builders of modern India. He was practically illiterate and spoke in a rustic dialect, yet the spiritual depth and power of his teachings impressed intellectual giants such as Friederich Max Muller. In Swami Vivekananda's estimation, his Master fully harmonized the intellectual, emotional, ethical, and spiritual elements of a human being and was the role model for the future.

3. Swami Vivekananda's family also provided a strong moral and cultural foundation to his life. Due in great part to

his upbringing, his tastes were eclectic and his interests wide. In fact, the desire for knowledge that he had acquired in his youth prompted him later to gather as much as he could wherever he was—whether in India or in the West.

4. Equally important, if not more so, was the Swami's knowledge of India based on his first-hand experiences acquired during his wanderings throughout the country. His pilgrimages transformed him. He became a true lover of humanity and became endowed with the quality of *sarvabhutahite ratāh* (being devoted to the welfare of all beings).[7]

At about the same time that Vivekananda completed his tour of India, he was asked to represent Hinduism at the World's Parliament of Religions, to be held that year (1893) in Chicago. Vivekananda also felt that this might give him an opportunity to do something for his country. So he agreed to go. When the Parliament of Religions convened in September 1893, Vivekananda created a sensation. While other delegates spoke of their own faiths and creeds, Vivekananda spoke of the God of all, the source and essence of every faith. His call for religious harmony and acceptance of all religions brought him great acclaim. When the Parliament was over, he went on a lecture tour in the Midwest and the East coast of the United States. People in large numbers, particularly intellectuals, came to hear him speak wherever he went, thus fulfilling his Master's prediction that he would some day become a 'world teacher.'

Vivekananda's tour of the United States also had a revitalizing effect on India. Previously, those who had gone to the West from India were full of apologies for the state of their country. He was not. He always spoke about his country with pride and respect. Thus, his work in the West instilled self-respect and self-confidence in the Indian psyche and helped India in its search for identity. It also helped to overcome the stereotypes and deep-rooted prejudices about India in Westerners' minds.

After giving up his lecture tour, the Swami started giving free classes on Vedanta and Yoga in New York. This resulted in the founding of the Vedanta Society there. In the summer of 1895 he sailed for England at the invitation of E. T. Sturdy and Henrietta Muller. His lectures there were quite successful. In December 1895 Vivekananda returned to the United States, where he continued his classes in New York and also lectured in other cities, and then returned to Europe again in April 1896. In May 1896, the Swami met Max Muller and his wife at Oxford. At the end of December 1896, Vivekananda sailed to India from Europe.

When the news broke that Swami Vivekananda was returning to India, people all over the country prepared to give him a hero's welcome. The Swami arrived in South India in January 1897 accompanied by three of his Western disciples. Wherever he went, addresses of welcome were presented and multitudes gathered to see him. In Vivekananda's response to these addresses, he indicated that he had a plan in mind to help uplift the masses. In fact, as early as 24 December 1894, he had written in a letter:

> My whole ambition in life is to set in motion a machinery which will bring noble ideas to the door of everybody, and then let men and women settle their own fate.[8]

On 1 May 1897, a few months after his return to Kolkata, the Swami set his plan in motion when he founded the Ramakrishna Mission. This was the beginning of an organized movement to help the suffering masses through educational, cultural, medical and relief work. Within a few weeks of the founding of the Ramakrishna Mission, one of Swami Vivekananda's brother disciples, Swami Akhandananda, was passing through Murshidabad in Bengal and was struck by the pitiful condition of the people there, who were suffering from a famine. He immediately started relief work. Since then the Ramakrishna Mission has continued to come to the aid of those suffering from natural or man-made calamities.

It may not be out of place to mention that in a speech made in 1993, Federico Mayor, Director-General of UNESCO, stated:

> I am indeed struck by the similarity of the constitution of the Ramakrishna Mission which Vivekananda established as early as 1897 with that of UNESCO drawn up in 1945. Both place the human being at the centre of their efforts aimed at development. Both place tolerance at the top of the agenda for building peace and democracy. Both recognize the variety of human cultures and societies as an essential aspect of the common heritage.[9]

About two years after Vivekananda's return to India, the centre, which his brother disciples had managed while he was in the West, was transferred to a large piece of land at Belur, across the river from Kolkata. This became the headquarters of the Ramakrishna Mission. Vivekananda emphasized that the aim of the mission was 'man-making', and he wanted it eventually to develop a university as part of its mission. About this time the Swami received a letter requesting him to head the Research Institute of Science that Sir Jamshedji Tata had set up, but he declined the offer as it conflicted with his spiritual interests.[10]

In June 1899, he returned to Europe with one of his brother disciples and also Sister Nivedita, an Irish disciple. After a short stay in London, Vivekananda sailed for New York. A few months later he left for California where a series of lectures and classes led to the founding of the Vedanta Society in San Francisco. He eventually returned to New York, but in July 1900 went to Paris, where he stayed for three months. During this time he participated in the Congress of the History of Religions held in connection with the Universal Exposition.

The Swami returned to Kolkata on 9 December 1900. For the most part he spent his last days at the Belur centre, training his young followers and guiding the organization. He expected his followers to be exemplars of an ideal type of human being, and he inspired them by saying:

> Tell me what you have done. Couldn't you give away one life for the sake of others?... Let this body go in the service of others—and then I shall know you have not come to me in vain![11]

On 4 July 1902, he was more vigorous than he had been for a long time, and he busied himself with various activities. In the evening he meditated and left his body, as he himself had predicted, in a high yogic state. He was only 39 years old.

Education—What It Means

Sister Nivedita used to say that those who knew Swami Vivekananda understood that he was one who had experienced in his own life all the truths about which he spoke. This is equally valid when he addressed the subject of education. Swamiji knew that education plays a vital role in curing the evils in society, and is critical in shaping the future of humanity. Although Vivekananda did not write a book on education, he contributed valuable thoughts on the subject that are relevant and viable today. In order to understand his thoughts, we should first consider his oft-quoted definition of education: 'Education is the manifestation of the perfection already in man.'[12]

Vivekananda's definition of education is one of remarkable insight. First of all, the word 'manifestation' implies that something already exists and is waiting to be expressed. The main focus in learning is to make the hidden ability of a learner manifest. As Vivekananda said, 'what a man "learns" is really what he "discovers", by taking the cover off his own soul, which is a mine of infinite knowledge.'[13] According to the Vedanta philosophy, knowledge is inherent in a human being, like a spark in a piece of flint, and all that is needed is the strike of suggestion to bring it out. 'Manifestation' indicates spontaneous growth, provided the impediments, if any, are removed.

Next in importance in the Swami's definition of education is the expression 'already in man.' This refers to a human being's potential, which is the range of the abilities and talents, known or unknown that he is born with. 'Potential' speaks of the possibility of awakening something that is lying dormant. Israel Scheffler, in his book *Of Human Potential*, considers three aspects of this:

(a) *the capacity* to acquire a specific characteristic or to become someone who possesses it. For instance, we might say, 'Amal has the capacity to become a Maradona, the world-famous soccer player';

(b) *the propensity* is an attribute which indicates what a person is likely to do when the opportunity comes and freedom of choice is available. It suggests something about a person's motivation. For example, Rabindranath Tagore's propensity, expressed in his *Gitanjali*, indicates his strong aspiration to discover the wonder behind this creation; and

2

(c) *the capability* means a person's motivation and efficiency in working towards an intended outcome. It refers to something more than a person's capacity to perform. Rather, it is a person's strength and capacity to get rid of obstacles to his learning—such as lack of motivation or obstacles in his environment.

Thus, these three concepts—capacity, propensity and capability—emphasize three aspects of education, respectively:

(a) That which makes learning possible;
(b) The development of learning; and
(c) Self-development or self-empowerment.

A child has many potentials of variable worth, and they may create mental conflict within him. Therefore, he has to learn to choose which he should try to develop, and which he should minimize, counter, or ignore. Then again, as his chosen potentials start to unfold, they should be supervized in order to achieve their harmonious and purposeful development.

The word 'perfection' in the Swami's definition of education is also very significant. We can see that every act connected with learning, training, etc., is part of a process directed towards an end. The English word 'perfect' implies completion, or something being made whole. The Greek word *teleics* is translated as 'perfect', and suggests the idea of attaining a goal or an end. Drawing on these meanings, one may conclude that perfection in educational parlance is the goal of actualizing the highest human potential.

The Goal of Education

The goal of education—general or ultimate—is essentially laid down by society and therefore varies from society to society. Even as every society tries to keep pace with the contemporary world, societies with a stable and older tradition cherish some higher goals of everlasting value. Taking into consideration the vast experience of the Indian civilization, Vivekananda's use of the word 'perfection' needs to be viewed at two levels:

1. 'Perfection' in the metaphysical sense implies the realization of the soul's own ever-perfect nature. The Vedanta philosophy says that a human being is not born a sinner, nor is he necessarily a victim of circumstances. The main cause of his suffering is his ignorance of his true nature. Explaining the implications of this, Vivekananda once said:

> The Light Divine within is obscured in most people. It is like a lamp in a cask of iron, no gleam of light can shine through. Gradually, by purity and unselfishness, we can make the obscuring medium less and less dense, until at last it becomes transparent as glass.[14]

2. At the empirical level, the concept of 'perfection' has to address the various problems human beings encounter in society. As Swami Vivekananda said:

> The education which does not help the common mass of people to equip themselves for the struggle for life, which does not bring out strength of character, a spirit of philanthropy, and the courage of a lion—is it worth the name? Real education is that which enables one to stand on one's own legs.[15]

Education, he said, must provide 'life-building, man-making, character-making assimilation of ideas.'[16] The ideal of this type of education would be to produce an integrated person—one who has learned how to improve his intellect, purify his emotions, and stand firm on moral virtues and unselfishness.

There are two levels of values designated by the ancient Indian scriptures, *parā vidyā* (spiritual values) and *aparā vidyā* (secular values). This division is merely for practical convenience; otherwise *vidyā*, or learning, is a continuum, leading one towards the ultimate goal which according to Vivekananda is complete freedom of the soul.

Vivekananda also observed that, if education is to serve the entire human being, in all his or her dimensions, the pursuit of knowledge will be a lifelong process. Even an illustrious person like Sri Ramakrishna said, from his own experience, 'As long as I live, so long do I learn.' At the empirical level, today's knowledge explosion can keep people engaged for their entire lives. Therefore, education must be considered a continuous and lifelong process.

Education and Social Justice

So far, our discussion of Vivekananda's ideas on education has been a simplistic analysis centring round his definition of education. However, this fails to do justice to some of his ideas on related issues, such as the relationship between education and society, between education and the teacher, between the professed goals of education and the goals actually achieved, and so forth. It is apparent, therefore, that Vivekananda's deep concern for social justice has not been so far reflected in our definition.

To this end, we can probe further into the expressions 'manifestation' and 'already in man,' bearing in mind the situation in India in those days. In explaining the term 'manifestation,' the Swami quoted part of one of the yoga aphorisms of Patanjali (4.3)—*Tatah kshetrikavat* (therefore the obstructions)—that is to say, just as a farmer breaks the barriers to a course of water, which thereafter flows by its own force to irrigate his fields, so also a person's inherent power will spontaneously manifest itself when external and internal obstacles, if any, are removed at the proper time by the teachers or the education system. Such obstacles are of various kinds. External obstacles might be in the form of unfair distribution of educational resources and opportunities, inequalities in economic development and socio-political instability; whereas internal obstacles might have to do with the dynamics of the education system, such as the teacher-student relationship, the student's capacity to make personal judgements or to adapt to changes, and the student's mental or physical capacities.

In order to tackle these obstacles, the education system should take on two responsibilities:

(a) It should help a person build a healthy and dynamic frame of mind to enable him to meet the challenges of life; and

(b) It should try to prevent, through proper training of its present students, any future evils in people and society which are likely to further complicate the problems of human beings.

At the same time, however, the teachers and the designers of education systems must always keep in mind the Vedantic idea that whatsoever good or bad impressions a mind carries, a human being is essentially pure and divine, and a repository of immense possibilities.

In Vivekananda's view, educational concerns related to a person's interaction with society should receive due attention. The purpose of society is to help secure the well-being of human beings. In reality, however, human beings frequently find themselves entrapped in a society that threatens their freedom, a freedom essential for their educational growth. An ideal society, according to Vivekananda, should provide the resources as well as the opportunity for each of its members to develop his or her potential to the maximum. Education must embrace the whole society, with special attention to those who are most in need of it and who, for one reason or another, are unable to avail themselves of the existing facilities.

Training the Mind

Vivekananda concurred with contemporary thinkers when he asserted that the mind—the chief instrument of learning—deserves more attention than it had earlier received. Training the mind should be a student's highest priority, and not simply the accumulation, the memorizing and the repeating of facts. In the long run, stuffing one's mind with information, technical skills and useless trivia only creates more problems if one's mind is not nourished and strengthened and made healthy. Yet training of the mind in all its aspects is conspicuously absent in today's education.

Learning to concentrate the mind was the focus in the Swami's scheme. He said:

> To me the very essence of education is concentration of mind, not the collecting of facts.[17]

In doing anything—such as thinking, working with the hands, etc.—the better the power of concentration the better the outcome will be. And this power of keeping the mind on the task can be improved. Training the mind to concentrate on a specific subject has several stages, the primary one being learning how to collect the mind and preventing it from running hither and thither. The student trains his mind to be more attentive and more 'mindful.'

Next, the student must learn how to detach his mind from distractions that impose themselves in spite of himself. Then, simultaneously, he must direct the mind to the desired subject and focus the full force of his mind on it. To give an example:

a convex lens gathers sunlight and focuses it on one point to burn a piece of paper. Likewise, when a mind becomes concentrated, it acquires tremendous power and is able to unlock the mysteries of the subject it is focused upon.

Similarly, the Swami also wanted students to cultivate will-power. According to him, will-power is developed when 'the current and expression of will are brought under control and become fruitful.'[18] Will-power is necessary not only to conduct the learning process, but also to strengthen one's character.

Culture and Education—The Teacher and the Pupil

Every society has its outer aspect called 'civilization,' and also its inner aspect called 'culture.' In both of these a child is moulded and educated so that the beliefs and practices of his forefathers are carried on and not forgotten. Nevertheless, as Vivekananda says:

> It is culture that withstands shocks, not a simple mass of knowledge. ... Knowledge is only skin-deep, as civilization is, and a little scratch brings out the old savage.[19]

A society is forever adding to its learning and culture. To the brilliant mind of T. S. Eliot, education was but a manifestation of culture. He said, 'The purpose of education, it seems, is to transmit culture; so culture is likely to be limited to what can be transmitted by education.'[20]

Similarly, Vivekananda observed that, through education, a child becomes cultured and his behaviour is moulded accordingly, and he is thus guided towards his eventual role in society. In this process, several agents—such as his parents, peers and teachers—assist him. But nowadays, as formal education has become more and more institutionalized, teachers are expected to play a more significant role. A teacher needs to help a student learn how to think, what to think, how to discriminate and how to appreciate things. This is not just a matter of intellectual manipulation. This kind of teaching requires moral conviction and the courage to continuously pursue one's own course at all costs. The teacher must not only possess the knowledge he is to transmit to the student, but he must also know how to transmit it. And in addition to the content of the teaching, what the teacher gives or transfers, to be truly effective, must possess some other elements. For instance, the teacher should share with the students the conviction that they are both truly one Spirit—at the same time cultivating in the student, a feeling of dignity and self respect.[21] As Vivekananda said:

> The only true teacher is he who can immediately come down to the level of the student, and transfer his soul to the student's soul and see through the student's eyes and hear through his ears and understand through his mind. Such a teacher can really teach and none else.[22]

In a favourable ambience such as this 'the process of uncovering'[23] the veil of ignorance works smoothly.

On the student's side, in order to facilitate manifestation of his innate strength and knowledge, he should cultivate the spirit of *śraddhā*—that is, faith in himself, humility, submission and veneration for the teacher. This is also necessary to create a favourable environment for learning. The *Taittiriya Upanishad* (1.11.2) gives the instruction: *Āchārya devo bhava*—let the teacher be your *deva* (i.e. a person fit to be worshipped or highly honoured). The teacher-pupil relationship, based on respect and mutual trust, is the cornerstone of the edifice of Vivekananda's scheme of education. The Upanishads also advocate this. Before starting the lesson, the teacher and the pupils were to pray together so that they would mutually benefit and be strengthened by the teaching/learning process.

Character Education and Universal Values

Vivekananda's guru, Sri Ramakrishna, used to say that *mānush* needs to become *mān-hush*—that is, a man needs to become a true man. 'He alone is a man,' he said, 'whose spiritual consciousness has been awakened'.[24] Following his Master, Vivekananda emphasized that 'the ideal of all education, all training, should be this man-making.' Lamenting over the prevailing system of education, he said:

> ... we are always trying to polish up the outside. What use in polishing up the outside when there is no inside? The end and aim of all training is to make the man grow.[25]

In order to rectify the defects in the existing system, man's limited view of himself, on which the existing system of education is based, needs to be reconsidered. A human being is not simply a composite of body and mind. He is something more. According to the Vedanta philosophy, a human being has five sheaths, or coverings: the physical sheath, the vital sheath, the mental sheath, the intellectual sheath, and the blissful sheath. Today's education can at best touch the first four sheaths, but not the last one. Secular knowledge, skills, and moral values may take care of the first four sheaths, but spiritual knowledge is essential for the fifth. Moreover, it should be noted that the fifth sheath is the reservoir of bliss, knowledge, and strength, and all the sheaths are activated by the fifth.

There is no doubt that today's education neglects training of the mind in all its aspects, but it also neglects the spiritual side of human beings. People's minds are not directed to higher pursuits of life with the result that their hidden potentials are not revealed. Only when wisdom, peace, strength, unselfishness, loving concern for others and other virtues become evident is a person transformed from a sensuous being to a true human being.

A tremendous explosion of knowledge without commensurate wisdom, plus immense power not tempered with discrimination, has made education today a potential source of danger. This is a serious problem looming large on humanity's horizon. As Vivekananda observed:

> Intellect has been cultured with the result that hundreds of sciences have been discovered, and their effect has been that the few have made slaves of the many—that is all the good that has been done. Artificial wants have been created; and every poor man, whether he has money or not, desires to have those wants satisfied, and when he cannot, he struggles, and dies in the struggle.[26]

In order to counterbalance this uneven development, Vivekananda strongly recommended the adoption of a 'spiritual and ethical culture,' and he looked upon 'religion as the innermost core of education.'[27] But by 'religion' he did not mean any particular religion. Religion to him meant the true eternal principles that inspire every religion. This is what touches the heart and has the potential to effect desirable changes in one's motivation. It also gives mental strength and broadness of outlook. Discussing the practical implications of morality, Swami Vivekananda once observed:

> What is meant by morality? Making the subject strong by attuning it to the Absolute, so that finite nature ceases to have control over us.[28]

Thus, in order to be worthwhile and effective, education must be rooted in religion—or, to be precise, in the science of spirituality, and evidently not in dogma.

Character-building was fundamental in Vivekananda's educational scheme, as against career-orientation, which occupies centre-stage in today's education. A person is what his thoughts have made him. Explaining this the Swami said, 'Each thought is a little hammer blow on the lump of iron which our bodies are, manufacturing out of it what we want it to be.'[29] That is why one finds that the focus of the Swami's educational thoughts was on assimilation of man-making, character-building ideas.

Everything a person does, every thought, every move, leaves an impression on the mind. Even when it is not outwardly apparent, it is strong enough to work beneath the surface. A person's character is determined by the sum total of these impressions. When a large number of these impressions come together, they form a habit. This then becomes a powerful force, for character is but repeated habits. This is why, through the acquisition and repetition of desirable habits, one's character can be remodelled.

The people one associates with, good or bad, contribute much to the development of one's character. In fact, their impact is greater than that of didactic teaching. That is why Swami Vivekananda said: 'Words, even thoughts, contribute only one-third of the influence in making an impression; the man, two-thirds.'[30] He therefore desired that the teacher's life and personality should be like a blazing fire which could have a positive influence on the pupils in his care. Exposure to exemplary role models, particularly when they are teachers, and also to wholesome curriculum materials that impart culturally-approved values to the young, is critical to character education.

Character-building education might focus on teaching what is right and wrong. But simultaneously, or alternatively, it should teach how to decide what is right and wrong. It has been rightly argued that participation in discussions of morality is more instructive than simply hearing about it. In any case, teachers should be moral exemplars if the classroom and the school are to serve as arenas for the teaching of ethics. The students then have the experience of being part of a group of people who take moral values seriously, and this helps them imbibe moral values spontaneously.

The present education system has overemphasized the cultivation of the intellect at the cost of the general well-being of humanity. To check this dangerous trend, Vivekananda strongly recommended all-round development of human beings. In one of his lectures he expressed the desire 'that all men were so constituted that in their minds *all* these elements of philosophy, mysticism, emotion, and of work were equally present in full! That is the ideal, my ideal of a perfect man.'[31]

And the Swami expected that the education systems would be suitably designed to produce such wholesome human beings. Interestingly, the UNESCO report *Learning to Be* published in 1972, while defining the aim of education, echoed this same idea. It reads: 'The physical, the intellectual, emotional and ethical integration of the individual into a complete man is a broad definition of the fundamental aim of education.'[32]

The Education System and the Poor

So far we have discussed education primarily in the context of the society that already benefits from education. Vivekananda, however, was a genuine friend of the poor and the weak, particularly the helpless masses of India, and he was the first Indian leader who sought a solution to their problems through education. He argued that a nation was advanced to the extent that education and culture reached the masses. Unless there was uniform circulation of national blood all over the body, the nation could not rise. He insisted that it was the duty of the upper classes, who had received their education at the expense of the poor, to come forward and uplift the poor through education and other means. In fact, the Swami's mission was for the poor. He once said, 'There must be equal chance for all—or if greater for some and for some less—the weaker should be given more chance than the strong.'[33]

The trend in recent years has been to shift the responsibility for education from the family, religious institutions, private charities and so forth, to public authorities, particularly the State. Yet, in spite of this shift to the State, education has hardly reached the most underprivileged. As they are often victims of malnutrition, poor hygienic conditions and overcrowded housing, they can hardly take advantage of any half-hearted opportunity that is offered.

Vivekananda felt that alienation of any kind from the masses of society, who are mostly poor—whether it be alienation through learning, through wealth or through force of arms—weakens the leadership of a county. Therefore, for a sustainable regeneration of India, if not for anything else, top priority must be given to educating the masses and restoring to them their lost individuality. They should not only be given education to make them self-reliant, but also ideas, moral training and an understanding of their own historical situation so that they can work out their own salvation. Furthermore, they must be given culture, without which there can be no hope for their long-term progress.

The Swami was particularly worried about the degradation of women in India. He was emphatic that women must be educated, for he believed that it is the women who mould the next generation, and hence, the destiny of the country. In Vivekananda's educational scheme for India, the uplift of women and the masses received the highest priority, and his ideas approximated to Paulo Freire's concept of 'Conscientization.'[34]

Conclusion

There have been many changes in the field of education since Swami Vivekananda passed away more than one hundred years ago, but not as many changes as in other areas of society. One such noticeable change in education is that it is now engaged in preparing human beings for a new type of society, and it is trying to create a new type of human being for it. Interestingly, Swami Vivekananda had envisioned a society with a new type of human being in whom knowledge, action, work, and concentration were harmoniously blended, and he proposed a new type of education for achieving this.

The right to education for everyone, guaranteed by the Constitution of India, was Vivekananda's dream, but it is still a far cry from its goal. His idea of continual or lifelong education, however, has been adopted in many countries already. Moreover, because of the adoption of continuous education in these countries, our idea of what constitutes success and failure has altered, raising new hope for the weak, underprivileged section of these societies—the very people who for various reasons cannot complete their education when they are young. Vivekananda's cry for the uplift of the downtrodden masses, particularly of the long-neglected women, has evoked a favourable response from different quarters, but societies tailor education to meet their own needs, thereby often robbing the weak of their freedom to determine their own destiny. Unless radical changes are made in all societies the poor will never be able to raise themselves. This was a major concern of the Swami.

There is a remarkable similarity between Vivekananda's thoughts and actions a century ago and the present concerns of UNESCO.

- His commitment towards universal values and tolerance, his active identification with humanity as a whole.
- The struggle in favour of the poor and destitute, to reduce poverty and to eliminate discrimination against women—reaching the unreached.
- His vision of education, science and culture as the essential instruments of human development.
- The idea that education should be a lifelong process.
- And the need to move away from rote learning.

Himself a visionary and an original thinker, Vivekananda pointed out in his first public lecture in Asia, on 15 January 1897: 'But education has yet to be in the world, and civilization—civilization has begun nowhere yet.'[35] This is true. If we consider civilization to be the manifestation of the divine in human beings, as Vivekananda conceived it to be, no society has made much progress so far. This is why we find that mildness, gentleness, forbearance, tolerance, sympathy and so forth—the signs of a healthy civilization—have not taken root in any society on an appreciable scale, although we prematurely boast of a global village. The lack of basic necessities among the underprivileged all over the world is no less striking than the lack of morality among the educated privileged ones. To squarely meet this great challenge, Vivekananda prescribed 'man-making and character-building education.'[36] For this reason, if not for anything else, Vivekananda's thoughts on education ought to be seriously re-examined today.

References and Notes

1. *Complete Works of Swami Vivekananda*, Advaita Ashrama, Kolkata [*hereafter*, CW] 4. 179.
2. *The Gospel of Sri Ramakrishna*, Sri Ramakrishna Math, Chennai [*hereafter*, Gospel] p. 35.

3. CW. 6.255.

4. CW. 8.476.

5. *Datta*, B. 1993. *Swami Vivekananda, Patriot-Prophet—A Study.* Kolkata: Nababharat Publishers. pp. 88, 286.

6. Gambhirananda, Swami. 1996. *Yuganayak Vivekananda*, 3 volumes (in Bengali), Kolkata: Udbodhan Karyalaya, Vol. I, p. 74.

7. *Bhagavad Gita,* 5.25.

8. CW. 5.29.

9. Speech by Federico Mayor, Director-General of UNESCO, on the occasion of the Exhibition and Seminar in Commemoration of the Centenary of Swami Vivekananda's appearance at the Parliament of Religions, Chicago, 1893, given at UNESCO Headquarters, 8 October 1993.

10. Vivekananda inspired Sir Jamshedji Tata to set up this educational scheme when they had travelled together from Yokohama to Chicago on the Swami's first visit to the West, in 1893.

11. Romain Rolland, *The Life of Vivekananda and the Universal Gospel*, trans. E. F. Malcolm-Smith (Kolkata: Advaita Ashrama, 1992), p. 166.

12. CW. 4.358.

13. CW. 1.28.

14. CW. 7.21.

15. CW. 7.147-148.

16. CW. 3.302.

17. CW. 6.38.

18. CW. 4.490.

19. CW. 3.291.

20. G. H. Bantock, *T. S. Eliot and Education.* London: Faber & Faber, 1970, p.86.

21. *Srimad Bhāgavatam*, 3.29.27.

22. CW. 4.183.

23. CW. 1.28.

24. Gospel, 851.

25. CW. 2.15.

26. CW. 1.414.

27. CW. 3.182; 5.231.

28. CW. 2.137.

29. CW. 7.20.

30. CW. 2.14.

31. CW. 2.388.

32. Edgar Faure et al., *Learning to Be,* Paris: UNESCO, 1972, p. 156.

33. *Letters of Swami Vivekananda*, p. 255.

34. Paulo Freire (1921-1997) of Brazil, one of the best known educators of our time, developed a teaching system based on an educational process that focuses on the learner's environment. According to Freire, the learner must be aware of the historical situation in which he is situated, and he must understand how the knowledge he acquires relates to himself and to the society he lives in. Freire laid emphasis on building critical awareness to enable a person to read and write not words, but true reality—i.e. to understand true reality. Critical awareness building does not stop at reflection but includes action on that reflection. Vivekananda also believed that a person is the maker of his own destiny and proper education can help him achieve this.

35. CW. 3.114.

36. In this connection we can cite the views of some historians. Will and Ariel Durant, in their *The Lessons of History*, said, 'Evolution in men during recorded time has been social rather than biological: it has proceeded not by heritable variations in the species, but mostly by economic, political, intellectual and moral innovation transmitted to individuals and generations by imitation, custom or education' (Will Durant and Ariel Durant, *The Lessons of History*, New York: Simon & Schuster, 1968, p. 34).

3

SWAMI VIVEKANANDA ON EDUCATION

We are all aware of the inadequacy of the present-day system of education. Educationists—Eastern and Western—are engaged for decades, in devising better methods of imparting knowledge and improving the morale of the student community. Despite their best efforts, we are, unfortunately, left in the same deplorable condition as we were before, and much worse, as is generally felt, there is a growing degeneration.

The reasons for the inadequacy and degeneration are quite obvious, but our savants of education are, for matters of policy and principle, not able to tackle the problems in their entirety.

Education in Ancient India

It is universally recognized that we had, in ancient India, a unique system of education, which attracted students from all over the then known world. But unable to appreciate the wealth of Indian culture, the foreign educationists considered it useless and even unhealthy, and so tried to replace it by their own. But we would forget it to our detriment that the architects of the glorious culture of this great land were saints and seers. It is to them that we have to turn for light and guidance in the apparently difficult endeavour of re-orientating the system of education in India.

It is singularly fortunate that one such saint-seer of India, Swami Vivekananda, has bestowed his thoughts on this difficult problem and has offered practical solutions, which, if zealously applied, will facilitate establishing a system that will be a harmonious blending of the culture of this land with the scientific methods of the West.

Even in the midst of his cyclonic activities the Swami clearly saw the defects of modern education which is a bundle of negations. He observed:

> The education that you are getting now has some good points, but it has a tremendous disadvantage which is so great that the good things are all weighed down. In the first place it is not a man-making education, it is merely and entirely a negative education. A negative education, or any training that is based on negation, is worse than death.[1]

But his was not a destructive criticism. He fully visualized the healthy system that is bound to replace the present one if India has to survive at all. So he said: 'We must have life-building, man-making, character-making assimilation of ideas.'[2]

This, in fact, is the *summum bonum* of education, an education which should aim at the development of the entire personality of man. The Swami has completely comprehended all the aspects of education, not neglecting its main purpose of imparting knowledge. So he has clarified: 'If you have assimilated five ideas and made them your life and character, you have more education than any man who has got by heart a whole library.'[3]

True Aim of Education

The object of the ideal system of education, then, should not merely be the advancement of theoretical knowledge but also the advancement of life, development of the highest powers and capacities, and the unfoldment of the noblest potentialities of the student. He must be enabled at the same time to apply intelligently to his own life all the ideas that he has learnt and gathered and thus promote his growth—physically, intellectually, morally, and spiritually.

Swami Vivekananda has tackled the problem in its entirety. Unlike those who try to paint and decorate a hopelessly dilapidated building in their vain efforts to make it new, this grand architect has suggested that a glorious mansion should be built on a firmer foundation. That is why he observes:

> Every improvement in India requires first of all an upheaval in religion. Before flooding the land with socialistic or political ideas, first deluge the land with spiritual ideas. If you attempt to get secular knowledge without religion, I tell you plainly, vain is your attempt in India; it will never have a hold on the people.[4]

The Role of Religion

The question arises as to why religion should be associated with education at all. The answer is obvious and more so in India.

The ordinary means of imparting education is to 'drive into the mind' of the student a mass of information for which he may possess no real interest. The child is ordinarily considered more or less a receiving machine. But according to the literal meaning of the term education, he is to be treated in an altogether different manner. He is to be regarded as a living entity with innate capacities and potentialities, which are to be drawn out.

'Whatever a man knows,' observes Swami Vivekananda, 'should, in strict psychological language, be what he discovers or unveils. What a man "learns" is really what he discovers by taking the cover off his soul.'[5]

In order to formulate any true system of education, we must first of all consider the nature of those whom we want to educate. Here a very important question arises: Are our children mere bodies—a mere, combination of cells—and their mind, an 'epiphenomenon'—a by-product of the highly organized brain cells—or, are they integrated body-minds? Or, are they spiritual entities, which move and dominate minds and bodies?

It is evident that a human being is not a mass of cells. He is a soul. We need not discuss here the superiority or otherwise of the different theories as to the true nature of human personality. But it is impossible to formulate any system of education without having a definite conception of the nature, the inner potentialities of the being we want to educate and train.

'Each soul', Swami Vivekananda declares, 'is potentially divine, and the goal is to manifest this divine within.'[6] He defines religion as 'the manifestation of the divinity already in man'.[7] This self-realization is possible only through education which is 'the manifestation of perfection already in man'.[8] The attainment of perfection brings out the divine nature. The goal of human existence is to manifest the perfection and divinity of the soul by removing the accretions and encrustations which have grown round what is taken to be the personality.

Growth of the Personality

But, with reference to the education of the child, we are not concerned with this ultimate nature and goal. We are now interested mainly in the child as a human being, and in the course he is to follow for the evolution and growth of his personality. It is enough for our present purpose if we regard the student under our care as a self-conscious entity, dwelling in the physical body, having organs of sense-perception and possessing the 'inner-organ' called the mind, with its faculties of intellect, feeling and will. These faculties are capable of being developed to the maximum tune of perfection. Associated with the mind, the self-conscious entity or spirit becomes a psychological being. Connected with the physical body, the psychological being becomes an embodied being—a human personality. Thus true education means an all-round culture—physical, intellectual, moral, and spiritual. A complete system of education cannot disregard any of these different aspects. It must take into account the development of a healthy body, a proper control of sense-impulses and instincts, the acquirement of knowledge, sublimation and proper direction of feeling and sentiment, development of the will and the sense of duty. It must have the rightful place for soul-culture which removes mental darkness and revives the glory of the pure self by enabling one to rise above the false personality founded on identification with the unreal and nourished by false desires and morbid gratification of the senses. The physical body is to be sustained by proper material food, the mind to be developed through the assimilation of the right type of ideas, and the soul, to be nourished by earnest prayer and meditation.

A complete system of education, as has been stated, implies a balance and harmony between the properly developed body, mind, and soul. Physical culture is comparatively simple and easy, while the culture of the mind is a more difficult affair as it has got its sub-conscious and conscious, its intuitive and intelligent processes with regard to the working of different faculties. The most difficult of all is the culture of the soul, which implies the awakening of the intuitive faculty or the soul's appreciation of itself and direct experience of the true Self, without passing through the complex, tortuous, and insufficient mental process. But, whatever it be, it will not do for us to evade a question which stares us in the face. In our attempt at formulating the right type of education, we have to regard life as an indivisible whole, and as such we have to include in our system of education both intellectual knowledge and spiritual realization.

Religion Ought to be the Basis

When the Swami perceived that religion should be the firm foundation on which the great edifice of education was to be built, he had in mind no particular religion, but a universal religion. So he said: 'I look upon religion as the innermost core of education. Mind, I do not mean my own or anybody else's opinion about religion. The true eternal principles have to be held before people.'[9]

In imparting religious education to the student, stress is to be laid on the essentials of one's faith, viz. the nature of the soul, its relation to the supreme Spirit and its attitude towards other souls. This is the basic common factor connecting all religions. It is to be distinguished from rituals and ceremonials which differ widely but help the student to realize the eternal relationship between his eternal soul and eternal God.

It is needless to say that only a pure and alert mind has the acumen to grasp instantaneously the instructions—secular and spiritual. The ancient Hindus with their incomparable knowledge of practical psychology laid proper stress on the prerequisites of an ideal studenthood. They had, of course, spiritual realization as the highest goal of life and made all secular knowledge subservient to it. But the path they prescribed for the attainment of knowledge holds equally good for receiving both the types, namely, secular and spiritual.

The Need for Brahmacharya

They held that the highest goal of life could be attained usually by passing through the various stages of life, one after another. Let us focus our attention on the first of them which is very pertinent with the issue with which we are dealing now. It is *brahmacharya*, the period of sense-control including practice of continence, mental discipline, and study. A *brahmachāri*, if he wants to take the vow of lifelong celibacy and finds himself fit for it, may remain as a *brahmachāri* without entering the family life at all. Or, he may take to the life of a hermit or that of a monk. But normally the youth, after he finds himself properly equipped for the struggles of life with its manifold distractions and temptations, should enter the stage of the householder. According to the Hindu ideal, marriage is a sacrament and the household is an *āshrama*—a place not for sense-gratification but for the performance of duties, worship, and service.

During the period of studentship, the foundation of life is to be laid properly. If it fails, later life is also bound to be a failure. That is the reason why great stress is laid on the life of *brahmacharya*. It was so in ancient times and it should be so in the present time also.

Speaking of the application of the ancient ideal of the student life to our present-day education, Swami Vivekananda observes: 'The old institution of living with the guru and such systems of imparting education are needed. What we want are Western science coupled with Vedanta, *brahmacharya* as guiding motto, and *śraddhā* and also faith in oneself.'[10]

The *Bhāgavatam* enumerates the duties of the *brahmachāri*:

The student must practice self-control and study the scriptures, along with other branches of learning. He should observe strict continence, never consciously departing from it. He must learn to offer his heart's worship to the Divine Self in all beings and to see the One God residing in all.[11]

Speaking of the power of continence, Sri Ramakrishna declares:

> If a man practices absolute *brahmacharya* for twelve years, the *medhā nādi* (nerve of intelligence) will open, i.e. ... his power of understanding will blossom. His understanding will become capable of penetrating and comprehending the subtlest ideas. With such an understanding man can realize God. God can be attained only through a purified understanding of this type.[12]

Chastity in thought, word, and deed, always and in all conditions, constitutes what is called *brahmacharya*. In it the energy that expresses itself as sexual energy, is transformed into spiritual energy. As Swami Vivekananda observes:

> The human energy which is expressed as sex-energy, in sexual thought, when checked and controlled, easily becomes changed into *ojas*. It is only the chaste man and woman who can make *ojas*, and store it in the brain; that is why chastity has always been considered the highest virtue. ...
>
> By the observance of strict *brahmacharya* all learning can be mastered in a very short time; one acquires unfailing memory of what one hears or knows but once. The chaste brain has tremendous energy and gigantic will-power.[13]

Modern Medical Men Support the Indian Ideal

This view is fully supported by the considered opinion of some eminent Western medical men. Observes one of them:

> It is a medical—a physiological—fact that the best blood in the body goes to form the elements of reproduction in both sexes. In a pure and orderly life, this matter is absorbed. It goes back into circulation, ready to form the finest brain,

nerve, and muscular tissue. This life of man, carried back and diffused through his system, makes him manly, strong, brave, and heroic. If wasted it leaves him effeminate, weak, and irresolute, intellectually and physically debilitated, and prey to sexual irritation, disordered function, morbid sensation, disordered muscular movement, a wretched nervous system, epilepsy, insanity, and death. The suspended use of the generative organs is attended with a notable increase of bodily vigour and spiritual life.[14]

In the words of many members of the medical profession of New York and its vicinity: 'Chastity, a pure continent life, is consonant with the best conditions of physical, mental, and moral health.'

Dr. Alexis Carrell, in his work, *Man the Unknown,* observes:

It is well known that sexual excesses impede intellectual activity. In order to reach its full power, intelligence seems to require both the presence of well-developed sexual glands and the temporary repression of the sexual appetite. Freud has rightly emphasized the capital importance of sexual impulses in the activities of consciousness. However his observations refer chiefly to sick people. His conclusions should not be generalized to include normal individuals, especially those who are endowed with a strong nervous system and a mastery over themselves. While the weak, the nervous, and the unbalanced become more abnormal when their sexual appetites are repressed, the strong are rendered still stronger by practising such a form of asceticism.[15]

To quote the words of two other authorities: 'For a young man up to the time of his marriage, chastity is most salutary, not only in an ethical and aesthetical sense, but also from hygienic standpoint.'

Mahatma Gandhi's Views on Brahmacharya

The goal of *brahmacharya* is to dwell in *Brahman* or attain spiritual realization. The means to attain it is an all-round sense-control and manifestation of the gathered energy along the line of spiritual striving and loving service, both of which lead the *brahmachāri* towards the highest illumination. In our modern world, Mahatma Gandhi advocated the practice of *brahmacharya* for the good of the individual and the family and society. He represents the ancient spirit of *brahmacharya* when he observes:

> Mere control of animal passion has been thought to be tantamount to observing *brahmacharya*. I feel that this conception is incomplete and wrong. *Brahmacharya* means control of all the organs of sense. He who attempts to control only one organ, and allows all the others free play, is bound to find his effort futile. To hear suggestive stories with the ears, to see suggestive sights with the eyes, to taste stimulating food with the tongue, to touch exciting things with the hands, and then at the same time to expect to control the only remaining organ is like putting one's hands in the fire, and expecting to escape being burnt. ... If we practice simultaneous self-control in all directions, the attempt will be scientific and possible of success.[16]

With a deep insight gained through his own striving and personal experience, he observes:

> Mind is at the root of all sensuality. ... Many aspirants after *brahmacharya* fail because in the use of their other sense-organs they want to carry on like those who are not

brahmachāris. Their effort is, therefore, identical with the effort to experience the bracing cold of winter in the scorching summer months.

Brahmacharya means control of the senses in thought, word and deed. ... So long as thought is not under complete control of the will *brahmacharya* in its fullness is absent. ... Curbing the mind is even more difficult than curbing the wind. Nevertheless the existence of God within makes even control of the mind possible.[17]

'Every boy,' declares Swami Vivekananda, 'should be trained to practice absolute *brahmacharya* and then *śraddhā*, faith, will come.'[18.]

Cultivation of Śraddhā *or Faith in Oneself*

The word *śraddhā* means faith in oneself, faith in Divine existence and grace, faith in the scriptures revealed to the sages, faith in one's potentialities and capacity for self-realization. In his inimitable way the Swami gives a new definition of the word *śraddhā*:

> The old religion said that he was an atheist who did not believe in God. The new religion says that he is an atheist who does not believe in himself. But it is not selfish faith. It means faith in all, because you are all. Love for yourself means love for all, for you are all. It is the greatest faith which will make the world better.[19]

As already pointed out, the Swami's ideal of education is based on the realization that man, in his essential nature, is Atman—pure Spirit. The body of ours is a *Devālaya*, the abode of the Divine Being. Just as the soul animates the body, God dwells as the Soul of all souls. It is the *Brahma Mandira*, the temple of *Brahman*, the supreme Spirit.

The indomitable energy of the youth is to be manifested not only in his studies and in attempts at self-mastery, but also in loving service to his fellow-beings. The education of a young man is never complete without his developing this sense of service.

References

1. *The Complete Works of Swami Vivekananda*, vol.3, 8th edn., p.301 (Henceforth CW.)

2. Ibid., p.302.

3. Ibid., p.302.

4. Ibid., p.302.

5. CW. 1.28. (10th edn)

6. Ibid., p.124.

7. CW. 4.358. (7th edn)

8. Ibid.

9. CW. 5.231. (7th edn)

10. Ibid., p.366.

11. *Srimad Bhāgavatam*, trans. Swami Prabhavananda, 1st edn., p.176.

12. *Sayings of Sri Ramakrishna*, 8th edn., p.170.

13. CW. 1.170. (10th edn)

14. Dr. Nicholls, *Esoteric Anthropology* quoted in *Bhakti-Yoga* by Ashwini Kumar Datta, p.62.

15. *Man the Unknown*, 8th edn., p.140.

16. From *Yervada Mandira*, 3rd edn., pp.13-14.

17. *My Experiments with Truth*, 4th edn., pp.258-59.

18. CW. 5.369. (7th edn)

19. CW. 2.301. (9th edn)

Swami Vivekananda as a Wandering Monk, Jaipur, 1891

Swami Vivekananda in Colombo, January, 1897

Swami Vivekananda at Oakland, February, 1900

PHILOSOPHY OF EDUCATION

Education is the manifestation of the perfection already in man. (CW. 4.358)

Knowledge is inherent in man. No knowledge comes from outside; it is all inside. What we say a man 'knows', should, in strict psychological language, be what he 'discovers' or 'unveils'; what a man 'learns' is really what he 'discovers', by taking the cover off his own soul, which is a mine of infinite knowledge.

We say Newton discovered gravitation. Was it sitting anywhere in a corner waiting for him? It was in his own mind; the time came and he found it out. ... The falling of an apple gave the suggestion to Newton, and he studied his own mind. He rearranged all the previous links of thought in his mind and discovered a new link among them, which we call the law of gravitation. It was not in the apple, nor in anything in the centre of the earth.

All knowledge, therefore, secular or spiritual, is in the human mind. In many cases it is not discovered, but remains covered, and when the covering is being slowly taken off, we say, 'We are learning.' (CW. 1.28)

What is education? Is it book-learning? No. Is it diverse knowledge? Not even that. The training by which the current and expression of will are brought under control and become

4

fruitful is called education. Now consider, is that education as a result of which the will, being continuously choked by force through generations, is well-nigh killed out; is that education under whose sway even the old ideas, let alone the new ones, are disappearing one by one; is that education which is slowly making man a machine? (CW. 4.490)

Education is not the amount of information that is put into your brain and runs riot there, undigested, all your life. We must have life-building, man-making, character-making as-similation of ideas. If you have assimilated five ideas and made them your life and character, you have more education than any man who has got by heart a whole library. ... If education is identical with information, the libraries are the greatest sages in the world, and encyclopaedias are the *rishis*.

(CW. 3.302)

Negative thoughts weaken men. Do you not find that where parents are constantly taxing their sons to read and write, telling them they will never learn anything, and calling them fools and so forth, the latter do actually turn out to be so in many cases? If you speak kind words to boys and encourage them, they are bound to improve in time. What holds good of children, also holds good of children in the region of higher thoughts. If you can give them positive ideas, people will grow up to be men and learn to stand on their own legs.

(CW. 7.170)

In language and literature, in poetry and the arts, in eve-rything we must point out not the mistakes that people are making in their thoughts and actions, but the way in which they will gradually be able to do these things better. Pointing out mistakes, wounds a man's feelings. (CW. 7.170)

You cannot teach a child anymore than you can grow a plant. All you can do is on the negative side—you can only help. It is a manifestation from within; it develops its own nature—you can only take away obstructions.   (CW. 5.410)

The education that you are getting now has some good points, but it has a tremendous disadvantage which is so great that the good things are all weighed down. In the first place it is not a man-making education, it is merely and entirely a negative education. A negative education or any training that is based on negation is worse than death.   (CW. 3.301)

We must have a hold on the spiritual and secular education of the nation. ... You must dream it, you must talk it, you must think it, and you must work it out. Till then there is no salvation for the race.   (CW. 3.301)

We must have the whole education of our country, spiritual and secular, in our own hands, and it must be on national lines, through national methods as far as practical. Of course this is a very big scheme, a very big plan. I do not know whether it will ever work out. But we must begin the work.

(CW. 3.302)

What is civilization? It is the feeling of the divine within.

(CW. 8.228)

Education has yet to be in the world, and civilization—civilization has begun nowhere yet.   (CW. 3.114)

The present system of education is all wrong. The mind is crammed with facts before it knows how to think.

(CW. 8.280)

Those of you who have read Herbert Spencer remember what he calls the 'monastery system' of education that was tried in Europe and which in some parts proved a success; that is, there is one schoolmaster, whom the village keeps. These primary schools are very rudimentary, because our methods are so simple. Each boy brings a little mat; and his paper, to begin with, is palm leaves. Palm leaves first, paper is too costly. Each boy spreads his little mat and sits upon it, brings out his inkstand and his books and begins to write. A little arithmetic, some Sanskrit grammar, a little of language and accounts—these are taught in the primary school.

(CW. 8.68)

The man at whose feet I sat all my life—and it is only a few ideas of his that I try to teach—could [hardly] write his name at all. All my life I have not seen another man like that, and I have travelled all over the world. When I think of that man, I feel like a fool, because I want to read books and he never did. He never wanted to lick the plates after other people had eaten. That is why he was his own book. All my life I am repeating what Jack said and John said, and never say anything myself. (CW. 6.64)

Books are infinite in number and time is short; therefore the secret of knowledge is to take what is essential. Take that and try to live up to it. (CW. 1.236)

It is one of the evils of your Western civilization that you are after intellectual education alone, and take no care of the heart. It only makes men ten times more selfish, and that will be your destruction. (CW. 1.412)

I would a hundred times rather have a little heart and no brain, than be all brains and no heart, ... he who has no heart and only brains dies of dryness. (CW. 2.145)

Bring light to the ignorant, and more light to the educated, for the vanities of the education of our time are tremendous! (CW. 3.247)

First of all comes the gift of food; next is the gift of learning, and the highest of all is the gift of knowledge. (CW. 7.159)

There is only one purpose in the whole of life—education. Otherwise what is the use of men and women, land and wealth? (CW. 8.431)

There are [more than] a hundred books comprising the Upanishads, some very small and some big, each a separate treatise. The Upanishads do not reveal the life of any teacher, but simply teach principles. They are [as it were] shorthand notes taken down of discussion in [learned assemblies], generally in the courts of kings. The word Upanishad may mean "sittings" [or "sitting near a teacher"]. (CW. 1.446)

Each nation is a type, physically and mentally. Each is constantly receiving ideas from others only to work them out into its type, that is, along the national line. The time has not come for the destruction of types. All education from any source is compatible with the ideals in every country; only they must be nationalized, i.e. fall in line with the rest of the type ... . (CW. 8.523-24)

SOCIETY AND EDUCATION

Well, you consider a man as educated if only he can pass some examinations and deliver good lectures. The education which does not help the common mass of people to equip themselves for the struggle for life, which does not bring out strength of character, a spirit of philanthropy and the courage of a lion—is it worth the name? Real education is that which enables one to stand on one's own legs. The education that you are receiving now in schools and colleges is only making you a race of dyspeptics. You are working like machines merely, and living a jelly-fish existence. (CW. 7.147-8)

Getting by heart the thoughts of others in a foreign language, and stuffing your brain with them and taking some university degrees, you consider yourself educated! Fie upon you! Is this education? What is the goal of your education? Either a clerkship, or being a roguish lawyer, or at the most a Deputy Magistracy, which is another form of clerkship—isn't that all? What good will it do you or the country at large? Open your eyes and see what a piteous cry for food is rising in the land of Bharata, proverbial for its wealth! Will your education fulfill this want? Never. (CW. 7.182)

We want that education by which character is formed, strength of mind is increased, the intellect is expanded, and by which one can stand on one's own feet. (CW. 5.342)

The training by which the current and expression of will are brought under control and become fruitful, is called education. (CW. 4.490)

It is man-making education all round that we want.
(CW. 3.224)

Education, education, education alone! Travelling through many cities of Europe and observing in them the comforts and education of even the poor people, there was brought to my mind the state of our own poor people, and I used to shed tears. What made the difference? Education was the answer I got. (CW. 4.483)

On one side, new India is saying, 'If we only adopt Western ideas, Western language, Western food, Western dress, and Western manners, we shall be as strong and powerful as the Western nations'; on the other, old India is saying, 'Fools! By imitation, others' ideas never become one's own; nothing, unless earned, is your own. Does the ass in the lion's skin become the lion?'

On one side, new India is saying, 'What the Western nations do is surely good, otherwise how did they become so great?' On the other side, old India is saying, 'The flash of lightning is intensely bright, but only for a moment; look out, boys, it is dazzling your eyes. Beware!' (CW. 4.477)

We have had a negative education all along from our boyhood. We have only learnt that we are nobodies. Seldom are we given to understand that great men were ever born in our country. Nothing positive has been taught to us. We do not even know how to use our hands and feet! ... We have learnt only weakness. (CW. 5.332)

The first duty is to educate the people. (CW. 3.216)

If you are to live at all, you must adjust yourself to the times. If we are to live at all, we must be a scientific nation.

(CW. 6.113)

Our part of the duty lies in imparting true education to all men and women in society. As an outcome of that education, they will of themselves be able to know what is good for them and what is bad, and will spontaneously eschew the latter. It will not be then necessary to pull down or set up anything in society by coercion. (CW. 6.493)

As to education and culture, it all depends upon the man. That is to say, where the men are highly cultured, there the women are; where the men are not, women are not.

(CW. 8.68)

Education for both boys and girls is neglected, entirely neglected. There are a great many things that should be done in that land (India). (CW. 8.70)

The only service to be done for our lower classes is to give them education, to develop their lost individuality. That is the great task between our people and princes. Up to now nothing has been done in that direction. (CW. 4.362)

The only way to bring about the levelling of caste is to appropriate the culture, the education, which is the strength of the higher castes. That done, you have what you want.

(CW. 3.291)

All the members of a society ought to have the same opportunity for obtaining wealth, education, or knowledge.

(CW. 5.146)

Now, from the oldest times, you know, the primary education, according to the old Hindu customs, belongs to the village system. All the land from time immemorial was nationalized ... belonged to the Government. There never is any private right in land. The revenue in India comes from the land, because every man holds so much land from the Government. This land is held in common by a community, it may be five, ten, twenty, or a hundred families. They govern the whole of the land, pay a certain amount of revenue to the Government, maintain a physician, a village schoolmaster, and so on.

(CW. 8.68)

The whole difference between the West and the East is in this: They are nations, we are not, i.e., civilization, education here is general, it penetrates into the masses. The higher classes in India and America are the same, but the distance is infinite between the lower classes of the two countries.

(CW. 8.306)

From the day when education and culture etc began to spread gradually from patricians to plebeians, grew the distinction between the modern civilization as of Western countries, and the ancient civilization as of India, Egypt, Rome, etc.

(CW. 4.482)

Set yourselves to the task of spreading education among the masses. ... Kindle their knowledge with the help of modern science. Teach them history, geography, science, literature, and along with these the profound truths of religion. In exchange for that teaching, the poverty of the teachers will also disappear. By mutual exchange both parties will become friendly to each other. (CW. 7.149)

Educate our people, so that they may be able to solve their own problems. Until that is done, all these ideal reforms will remain ideals only. (CW. 5.215)

If ever I get money in my possession, I shall first spend that in the service of man. Man is first to be saved; he must be given food, education, and spirituality. (CW. 6.451)

Yonder plot of land on the south side of the Math will be the center of learning, where grammar, philosophy, science, literature, rhetoric, the *Śrutis*, *Bhakti* scriptures, and English will be taught. ... Teaching will be imparted here irrespective of caste or creed, and those who will have objection to this will not be admitted. (CW. 7.158)

The ideal of all education, all training, should be this man-making. But, instead of that, we are always trying to polish up the outside. What use in polishing up the outside when there is no inside? The end and aim of all training is to make the man grow. The man who influences, who throws his magic, as it were, upon his fellow-beings, is a dynamo of power, and when that man is ready, he can do anything and everything he likes; that personality put upon anything will make it work. (CW. 2.15)

Why does not the nation move? First educate the nation, create your legislative body, and then the law will be forthcoming. First create the power, the sanction from which the law will spring. The kings are gone; where is the new sanction, the new power of the people? Bring it up. Therefore, even for social reform, the first duty is to educate the people, and you will have to wait till that time comes. (CW. 3.216)

Most of the monks are educated. Those that are not are also having secular education. But above all, to do good, perfect unselfishness is absolutely necessary. (CW. 8.424)

We get mostly those who have already educated themselves. What is needed is training them into our method and building up of character. The training is to make them obedient and fearless; and the method is to help the poor physically first and then work up to higher regions of mentality.

(CW. 8.425)

Are not drums made in the country? Are not trumpets and kettle-drums available in India? Make the boys hear the deep-toned sound of these instruments. Hearing from boyhood the sound of these effeminate forms of music and the listening to the *kirtana*, the country is well-nigh converted into a country of women. ... The *damaru* and horn have to be sounded; drums are to be beaten so as to raise the deep and martial notes.

(CW. 7.232-3)

It is one of the evils of your Western civilization that you are after intellectual education alone, and take no care of the heart. It only makes men ten times more selfish. ... When there is conflict between the heart and the brain, let the heart be followed. ... It is the heart which takes one to the highest plane, which intellect can never reach; it goes beyond intellect, and reaches to what is called inspiration. (CW. 1.412-3)

Always cultivate the heart. (CW. 1.415)

From the highest God to the meanest grass, the same power is present in all—whether manifested or not. We shall have to call forth that power by going from door to door.

... Along with this, education has to be imparted. That is easy to say, but how to reduce it into practice? There are thousands of unselfish, kind-hearted men in our country who have renounced everything. In the same way as they travel about and give religious instructions without any remuneration, so at least half of them can be trained as teachers or bearers of such education as we need most. For that, we want first of all a centre in the capital of each Presidency, from whence to spread slowly throughout the whole of India. Two centres have recently been started in Madras and Kolkata; there is hope of more soon. Then, the greater part of the education to the poor should be given orally, time is not yet ripe for schools. Gradually in these main centres will be taught agriculture, industry, etc., and workshops will be established for the furtherance of arts. To sell the manufactures of those workshops in Europe and America, associations will be started like those already in existence. It will be necessary to start centres for women, exactly like those for men.   (CW. 4.484-5)

In our books there is the doctrine of universal equality, but in work we make great distinctions. It was in India that unselfish and disinterested work of the most exalted type was preached; but in practice we are awfully cruel, awfully heartless—unable to think of anything besides our own mass-of-flesh bodies.
                                                    (CW. 5.127)

About the psychical things that have been the subject of discussion, I have very little to say here, for in the first place, the question is whether psychical subjects are capable of scientific demonstration. What do you mean by this demonstration?

First of all, there will be the subjective and the objective side necessary. Taking chemistry and physics, with which we are so familiar, and of which we have read so much, is it true that everyone in this world is able to understand the demonstration even of the commonest subjects? Take any boor and show him one of your experiments. What will he understand of it? Nothing. It requires a good deal of previous training to be brought up to the point of understanding an experiment. Before that he cannot understand it at all. That is a great difficulty in the way. If scientific demonstration means bringing down certain facts to a plane which is universal for all human beings, where all beings can understand it, I deny that there can be any such scientific demonstration for any subject in the world. If it were so, all our universities and education would be in vain. Why are we educated if by birth we can understand everything scientific? Why so much study? It is of no use whatsoever. (CW. 4.192-3)

Our character has disappeared. Our English education has destroyed everything and left nothing in its place. Our children have lost their politeness. To talk nicely is degrading. To be reverential to one's elders is degrading. Irreverence has been the sign of liberty. It is high time that we go back to our old politeness. The reformers have nothing to give in place of what they have taken away. Yet in spite of the most adverse surrounding of climate, etc., we have been able to do much, we have to do much more. I am proud of my race, I do not despair, (and) I am seeing daily a glorious and wonderful future in my mental visions. Take greatest care of these young ones on whom our future depends. (CW. 9.546-7)

THE TRUE TEACHER

In regard to the teacher, we must see that he knows the spirit of the scriptures. The whole world reads Bibles, Vedas and Korans; but they are all only words, syntax, etymology, philology, the dry bones of religion. The teacher who deals too much in words and allows the mind to be carried away by the force of words loses the spirit. It is the knowledge of the spirit of the scriptures alone that constitutes the true religious teacher.

(CW. 3.48-9)

The second condition necessary in the teacher is—sinlessness. The question is often asked, 'Why should we look into the character and personality of a teacher?'... This is not right... The sine qua non of acquiring. ... truth for one's self or for imparting to others is the purity of heart and soul. ... He must be perfectly pure, and then alone comes the value of his words.   (CW. 3.50)

The function of the teacher is indeed an affair of the transference of something, and not one of mere stimulation of the existing intellectual or other faculties in the taught. Something real and appreciable as an influence comes from the teacher and goes to the taught. Therefore the teacher must be pure.

(CW. 3.50-1)

The only true teacher is he who can convert himself, as it were, into a thousand persons at a moment's notice. The only true teacher is he who can immediately come down to the level of the student, and transfer his soul to the student's soul and see through the student's eyes and hear through his ears and understand through his mind. Such a teacher can really teach and none else. All these negative, breaking-down, destructive teachers that are in the world can never do any good.

(CW. 4.183)

No one was ever really taught by another; each of us has to teach himself. The external teacher offers only the suggestion which rouses the internal teacher to work to understand things. (CW. 1.93)

My idea of education is personal contact with the teacher—*gurugriha-vāsa*. Without the personal life of a teacher there would be no education. (CW. 5.224)

THE TEACHER AND THE TAUGHT

One should live from his very boyhood with one whose character is like a blazing fire and should have before him a living example of the highest teaching. (CW. 5.369)

The old system of education in India... is very different from the modern system. The students had not to pay. It was thought that knowledge is so sacred that no man ought to sell it. Knowledge must be given freely and without any price. The teachers used to take students without charge, and not only so, most of them gave their students food and clothes. To support these teachers the wealthy families... made gifts to them... and they in their turn had to maintain their students.

(CW. 4.162-3)

There are certain conditions necessary in the taught, and also in the teacher. The conditions necessary in the taught are purity, a real thirst after knowledge, and perseverance.

(CW. 4.24)

Purity in thought, speech, and act is absolutely necessary. ... As to the thirst after knowledge, it is an old law that we all get whatever we want. None of us can get anything other than what we fix our hearts upon. ... There must be a continuous struggle, a constant fight, an unremitting grappling with our lower nature, till the higher want is actually felt and victory is achieved. ... The student who sets out with such a spirit of perseverance will surely find success and realization at last.

(CW. 3.48)

With the teacher, therefore, our relationship is the same as that between an ancestor and his descendant. Without faith, humility, submission, and veneration in our hearts towards our religious teacher, there cannot be any growth of religion in us. ... In those countries which have neglected to keep up this kind of relation the religious teacher has become a mere lecturer, the teacher expecting his five dollars and the person taught expecting his brain to be filled with the teacher's words, and each going his own way after this much has been done.

(CW. 3.52)

The true teacher is one who can throw his whole force into the tendency of the taught. Without real sympathy we can never teach well. (CW. 7.99)

You see, no one can teach anybody. The teacher spoils everything by thinking that he is teaching. Thus Vedanta says that within man is all knowledge—even in a boy it is so—and it requires only an awakening, and that much is the work of a teacher. We have to do only so much for the boys that they may learn to apply their own intellect to the proper use of their hands, legs, ears, eyes, etc. and finally everything will become easy. (CW. 5.366)

The bond between the teacher and the taught ... is peculiar to India. The teacher is not a man, who comes just to teach me, and I pay him so much, and there it ends. In India it is really like an adoption. The teacher is more than my own father, and I am truly his child, his son in every respect. I owe him obedi-

5

ence and reverence first, before my own father even; because, they say, the father gave me this body, but he showed me the way to salvation, he is greater than father. And we carry this love, this respect for our teacher all our lives.

(CW. 8.78)

The disciple must have faith in the guru (teacher). In the West the teacher simply gives intellectual knowledge; that is all. The relationship with the teacher is the greatest in life. My dearest and nearest relative in life is my guru; next, my mother; then my father. My first reverence is to the guru.

(CW. 8.112)

He alone teaches who has something to give, for teaching is not talking, teaching is not imparting doctrines, it is communicating. (CW. 4.177-8)

Find the (spiritual) teacher, serve him as a child, open your heart to his influence, see in him God manifested.

(CW. 4.28)

There are still greater dangers in regard to the transmitter, the guru (spiritual teacher). There are many who, though immersed in ignorance, yet, in the pride of their hearts, fancy they know everything, and not only do not stop there, but offer to take others on their shoulders; and thus the blind leading the blind, both fall into the ditch. ... The world is full of these. Every one wants to be a teacher; every beggar wants to make a gift of a million dollars! Just as these beggars are ridiculous, so are these teachers. (CW. 3.47)

The old institution of 'living with the guru' and similar systems of imparting education are needed. What we want are western science coupled with Vedanta, *brahmacharya* as the guiding motto, and also *śraddhā* and faith in one's own self. Another thing that we want is the abolition of that system which aims at educating our boys in the same manner as that of the man who battered his ass, being advised that it could thereby be turned into a horse. (CW. 5.366)

You cannot make a plant grow in soil unsuited to it. A child teaches itself. But you can help it to go forward in its own way. What you can do is not of the positive nature, but of the negative. You can take away the obstacles, but knowledge comes out of its own nature. Loosen the soil a little, so that it may come out easily. Put a hedge round it; see that it is not killed by anything, and there your work stops. You cannot do anything else. The rest is a manifestation from within its own nature. So with the education of a child; a child educates itself. (CW. 4.55)

All teaching implies giving and taking, the teacher gives and the taught receives, but the one must have something to give, and the other must be open to receive. (CW. 4.178)

The teaching must therefore be modified according to the needs of the taught. ... Fire a mass of bird-shot, one at least will strike; give a man a whole museum of truths, he will at once take what is suited to him. Past lives have moulded our tendencies; give to the taught in accordance with his tendency. Intellectual, mystical, devotional, practical—make one the basis, but teach the others with it. (CW. 7.98)

EDUCATION OF THE MASSES

The great national sin is the neglect of the masses, and that is one of the causes of our downfall. No amount of politics would be of any avail until the masses in India are once more well educated, well fed, and well cared for.   (CW. 5.222-3)

A nation is advanced in proportion as education and intelligence spread among the masses. The chief cause of India's ruin has been the monopolizing of the whole education and intelligence of the land... among a handful of men. If we are to rise again, we shall have to do it... by spreading education among the masses.   (CW. 4.482)

The only service to be done for our lower classes is to give them education, to develop their lost individuality. ... They are to be given ideas; their eyes are to be opened to what is going on in the world around them; and then they will work out their own salvation. Every nation, every man, and every woman must work out their own salvation. Give them ideas—that is the only help they require and then the rest must follow as the effect. Ours is to put the chemicals together, the crystallization comes in the law of nature.   (CW. 4.362)

The great difficulty in the way of educating the poor is this. Supposing even your Highness (Maharaja of Mysore) opens a free school in every village, still it would do no good, for the poverty in India is such, that the poor boys would rather go to help their fathers in the fields, or otherwise try to make a living, than come to the school. Now if the mountain does not come to Mohammed, Mohammed must go to the mountain. If the poor boy cannot come to education, education must go to him. There are thousands of single-minded, self-sacrificing *sannyāsins* in our own country, going from village to village, teaching religion. If some of them can be organized as teachers of secular things also, they will go from place to place, from door to door, not only preaching, but teaching also. Suppose two of these men go to a village in the evening with a camera, a globe, some maps, etc. They can teach a great deal of astronomy and geography to the ignorant. By telling stories about different nations, they can give the poor a hundred times more information through the ear than they can get in a lifetime through books. (CW. 4.363)

Engrossed in the struggle for existence, they (the lower classes) had not the opportunity for the awakening of knowledge. They have worked so long uniformly like machines... and the clever educated section have taken the substantial part of the fruits of their labour. ... But times have changed. The lower classes are gradually awakening to this fact and making a united front against this... The upper classes will no longer be able to repress the lower, try they ever so much. The well-being of the higher classes now lies in helping the lower to get their legitimate rights. Therefore, I say, set yourselves to the task of spreading education among the masses. Tell them and make them understand, 'You are our brothers—a part and parcel of our bodies,'... If they receive this sympathy from you, their enthusiasm for work will be increased a hundredfold.

(CW. 7.148-9)

If the poor cannot come to education, education must reach them at the plough, in the factory, everywhere. (CW. 8.308)

How can there be any progress of the country without the spread of education, the dawning of knowledge? Even no real effort or exertion in the cause is visible among the few in your country who are the promise of the future, you who have received the blessings of education. But know for certain that absolutely nothing can be done to improve the state of things, unless there is spread of education first among the women and the masses. (CW. 6.489)

My whole ambition in life is to set in motion a machinery which will bring noble ideas to the door of everybody, and then let men and women settle their own fate. Let them know what our forefathers as well as other nations have thought on the most momentous questions of life. Let them see specially what others are doing now, and then decide. (CW. 5.29)

We must have a hold on the spiritual and secular education of the nation. ... You must dream it, you must talk it, you must think it, and you must work it out. (CW. 3.301)

Intelligence must not remain the monopoly of the cultured few; it will be disseminated from higher to lower classes. Education is coming, and compulsory education will follow.
(CW. 5.199)

I call him a traitor who, having been educated, nursed in luxury by the heart's blood of the downtrodden millions of toiling poor, never even takes a thought for them.
(CW. 8.329-30)

You must get together a number of poor, indigent folk. Having done all this, show them pictures to teach them astronomy, geography, etc., ... Try to have their eyes opened as to what has taken place or is taking place in different countries, what this world is like and, so forth. You have got lots of poor and ignorant folk there. Go to their cottages, from door to door, in the evening, at noon, any time—and open their eyes. Books etc., won't do—give them oral teaching.   (CW. 6.289-90)

Educate and raise the masses, and thus alone a nation is possible. Our reformers do not see where the wound is, they want to save the nation by marrying the widows; do you think that a nation is saved by the number of husbands its widows get? ... The real nation who live in cottage have forgotten their manhood, their individuality. Trodden under the foot of the Hindu, Mussulman, or Christian, they have come to think that they are born to be trodden under the foot of everybody who has money enough in his pocket. They are to be given back their lost individuality. They are to be educated. ... How? You have seen my brethren. Now I can get hundreds of such, all over India, unselfish, good and educated. Let these men go from village to village bringing not only religion to the door of everyone but also education. So I have a nucleus of organizing the widows also as instructors to our women.

(CW. 8.307-8)

India is to be raised, the poor are to be fed, education is to be spread, and the evil of priestcraft is to be removed.

(CW. 4.368)

If there is inequality in nature, still there must be equal chance for all—or if greater for some and for some less—the weaker should be given more chance than the strong. In other words, a brahmin is not so much in need of education as a *chandāla*. If the son of a brahmin needs one teacher, that of a *chandāla* needs ten. For, greater help must be given to him whom nature has not endowed with an acute intellect from birth.

(CW. 6.319)

There is some chance if you can impart education to the masses. Is there a greater strength than that of knowledge? Can you give them education? Name me the country where rich men ever helped anybody! In all countries it is the middle classes that do all great works. (CW. 6.325)

It is culture that withstands shocks, not a simple mass of knowledge. ... We all know in modern times of nations, which have masses of knowledge, but what of them? They are like tigers; they are like savages, because culture is not there. Knowledge is only skin-deep, as civilization is, and a little scratch brings out the old savage. Such things happen; this is the danger. Teach the masses in the vernaculars, give them ideas; they will get information, but something more is necessary; give them culture. Until you give them that, there can be no permanence in the raised condition of the masses. (CW. 3.291)

All the members of a society ought to have the same opportunity for obtaining wealth, education, or knowledge. The second question is: those who say that if the ignorant and the poor be given liberty, i.e. full right to their body, wealth, etc., and if their children have the same opportunity to better their condition and acquire knowledge as those of the rich and the highly situated, they would become perverse—do they say this for the good of society or blinded by their selfishness? In England too I have heard, 'Who will serve us if the lower classes get education?' (CW. 5.146)

EDUCATING THE WOMEN

They [women] have many and grave problems, but none that
are not to be solved by that magic word 'education'.

(CW. 5.231)

Brahmachāriṇis of education and character should take up the
task of teaching. (CW. 6.489)

In villages and towns they will open centres and strive for the
spread of female education. Through such devout preachers
of character there will be the real spread of female education
in the country. (CW. 7.217-8)

History and the *Purāṇas*, housekeeping and the arts, the duties
of home life and principles that make for the development of
an ideal character have to be taught. (CW. 6.489)

Other matters such as sewing, culinary art, rules of domestic
work, and upbringing of children, will also be taught while
japa, worship, and meditation shall form an indispensable
part of the teaching. (CW. 7.217)

Along with other things they should acquire the spirit of
valour and heroism. In the present day it has become necessary for them also to learn self-defence. (CW. 5.342)

With such an education women will solve their own problems. They have all the time been trained in helplessness, servile dependence on others and so they are good only to weep their eyes out at the slightest approach of a mishap or danger.

(CW. 5. 342)

Educate your women first and leave them to themselves; then they will tell you what reforms are necessary for them.

(CW. 6.115)

One does not find any real endeavour in your country to get the women educated. You, the men, are educating yourselves to develop your manhood, but what are you doing to educate and advance those who share all your happiness and misery, who lay down their lives to serve you in your homes?

(CW. 6.488)

How many schools have been started on your own national lines...? But alas, such a system does not obtain even among the men of your country, what to speak of women! It is seen from the official statistics that only three or four per cent of the people in India are educated, and not even one per cent of the women.

(CW. 6.488-9)

Religion, arts, science, housekeeping, cooking, sewing, hygiene—the simple essential points in these subjects ought to be taught to our women. ... The Mahākāli Pāṭaśālā is to a great extent moving in the right direction. But only teaching rites of worship won't do; their education must be an eye-opener in all matters. Ideal characters must always be presented before the view of the girls to imbue them with a devotion to lofty principles of selflessness. The noble examples of Sitā, Sāvitri, Damayanti, Lilāvati, Khana and Mirā should be brought home to their minds, and they should be inspired to mould their own lives in the light of these. (CW. 6.493-4)

In these modern days there is a greater impetus towards higher education on the European lines, and the trend of opinion is strong towards women getting this higher education. Of course, there are some people in India who do not want it, but those who do want it carried the day. It is a strange fact that Oxford and Cambridge are closed to women today, so are Harvard and Yale; but Kolkata University opened its doors to women more than twenty years ago. I remember that the year I graduated, several girls came out and graduated—the same standard, the same course, the same in everything as the boys; and they did very well indeed. (CW. 8.69)

I should very much like our women to have your intellectuality, but not if it must be at the cost of purity [stated in New York]. I admire you for all that you know, but I dislike the way that you cover what is bad with roses and call it good. Intellectuality is not the highest good. Morality and spirituality are the things for which we strive. (CW. 5.412)

I have it in my mind to train up some *brahmachārins* and *brahmachāriṇis*, the former of whom will eventually take the vow of *sannyāsa* and try to carry the light of education among the masses, from village to village, throughout the country, while the latter will do the same among women. But the whole work must be done in the style of our own country. Just as centres have to be started for men, so also centres have to be started for teaching women. ... Principles that make for the development of an ideal character have to be taught with the help of modern science, and the women students must be trained up in ethical and spiritual life. We must see to their ' growing up as ideal matrons of home in time. The children of such mothers will make further progress in the virtues that distinguish the mothers. (CW. 6.489)

To make a beginning in women's education: our Hindu women easily understand what chastity means, because it is their heritage. Now, first of all, intensify that ideal within them above everything else, so that they may develop a strong character by the force of which, in every stage of their life, whether married, or single if they prefer to remain so, they will not be in the least afraid even to give up their lives rather than flinch an inch from their chastity. Is it little heroism to be able to sacrifice one's life for the sake of one's ideal, whatever that ideal may be? (CW. 5.342-3)

Women must be put in a position to solve their own problems in their own way. No one can or ought to do this for them. And our Indian women are as capable of doing it as any in the world. (CW. 5.229-30)

It is only in the homes of educated and pious mothers that great men are born. And you have reduced your women to something like manufacturing machines; alas, for heaven's sake, is this the outcome of your education? The uplift of the women, the awakening of the masses must come first, and then only can any real good come about for the country, for India. (CW. 6.489-90)

How far is the birthplace of this venerable lady (referring to Tapasvini Mātāji of Mahākāli Pāṭaśālā)! She has renounced everything of her worldly life, and yet how diligent in the service of humanity! Had she not been a woman, could she ever have undertaken the teaching of women in the way she is doing? What I saw here was all good, but that some male householders should be pitch-forked as teachers is a thing I cannot approve of. The duty of teaching in the school ought to devolve in every respect on educated widows and *brahmachāriṇis.* (CW. 6.490-1)

In India alone the sight of feminine modesty and reserve soothes the eye! With such materials of great promise, you could not, alas, work out their uplift! You did not try to infuse the light of knowledge into them! If they get the right sort of education, they may well turn out to be ideal women in the world. (CW. 6.491)

These celibate nuns will in time be the teachers and preachers of the Math. In villages and towns they will open centers and strive for the spread of female education. Through such devout preachers of character there will be the real spread of female education in the country. (CW. 7.217-8)

They must be given education and left to themselves. After that they will act as they think best. Even after marriage and entering the world, the girls (so) educated will inspire their husbands with noble ideals and be the mothers of heroic sons. (CW. 7.218)

I ask you all so earnestly to do likewise and open girls' schools in every village and try to uplift them. If the women are raised, then their children will by their noble actions glorify the name of the country—then will culture, knowledge, power, and devotion awaken in the land. (CW. 7.220)

Biligiri has two widowed daughters. Kindly educate them and make special efforts that through them more such widowed women get a thorough grounding in their own religion and learn a little English and Sanskrit. (CW. 8.397)

Disciple: But, Sir, contrary results appear to have come out of the present female education. With just a smattering of education, they take merely to the Western modes of living.

Swamiji: In the beginning a few mistakes like that are unavoidable. When a new idea is preached in the country, some, failing to grasp it properly, go wrong in that way. But what matters it to the well-being of society at large? Well, those who are pioneers of the little bit of female education that now obtains in the country were undoubtedly very great-hearted. But the truth is that some defect or other must creep into that learning or culture which is not founded on a religious basis. But now female education is to be spread with religion as its centre. All other training should be secondary to religion. Religious training, the formation of character and observance of the vow of celibacy—these should be attended to. In the female education which has obtained up till now in India, it is religion that has been made a secondary concern, hence those defects you were speaking of have crept in. But no blame attaches therefore to the women. (CW. 7.220-1)

I have never seen women elsewhere as cultured and educated as they are here[in America]. Well-educated men there are in our country, but you will scarcely find anywhere women like those here. It is indeed true, that 'the Goddess Herself lives in the houses of virtuous men as Lakshmi'. I have seen thousands of women here whose hearts are as pure and stainless as snow. Oh, how free they are! It is they who control social and civic duties. Schools and colleges are full of women, and in our country women cannot be safely allowed to walk in the streets! ... And how pure and chaste are they here! Few women are married before twenty or twenty-five and they are as free as the birds in the air. They go to market, school, and college, earn money, and do all kinds of work. Those who are well-to-do devote themselves to doing good to the poor. And what are we doing? We are very regular in marrying our girls at eleven years of age lest they should become corrupt and immoral. What does our Manu enjoin? 'Daughters should be supported and educated with as much care and attention as the sons'. As sons should be married after observing *brahmacharya* up to the thirtieth year, so daughters also must observe *brahmacharya* and be educated by their parents. But what are we actually doing? Can you better the condition of your women? Then there will be hope for your well-being. Otherwise you will remain as backward as you are now. (CW. 5.25-6)

LANGUAGE

We haven't even got a single book well suited for the little boys. ... We must compose some books... with short stories from the *Rāmāyaṇa*, the *Mahābhārata*, the Upanishads, etc., in very easy and simple language, and these are to be given to our little boys to read. (CW. 5.371)

The greatness of a teacher consists in the simplicity of his language. (CW. 5.106)

'Arise, awake, sleep no more; within each of you there is the power to remove all wants and all miseries. Believe this, and that power will be manifested.' Teach this to all, and, with that, spread among the masses in plain language the central truths of science, philosophy, history, and geography. I have a plan to open a centre with the unmarried youths; first of all I shall teach them, and then carry on the work through them.
(CW. 6.454)

Simplicity is the secret. My ideal of language is my Master's language, most colloquial and yet most expressive. It must express the thought which is intended to be conveyed.
(CW. 5.259)

The Bengali language must be modelled not after the Sanskrit, but rather after the Pāli, which has a strong resemblance to it. In coining or translating technical terms in Bengali, one must, however, use all Sanskrit words for them, and an attempt should be made to coin new words. For this purpose, if a collection is made from a Sanskrit dictionary of all those technical terms, then it will help greatly the constitution of the Bengali language. (CW. 5.259)

6

THE MOTHER TONGUE

You will understand the difficulty when I tell you that I have been studying this language (Sanskrit) all my life, and yet every new book is new to me. How much more difficult would it then be for people who never had time to study the language thoroughly! Therefore the ideas must be taught in the language of the people.   (CW. 3.290)

Every man is capable of receiving knowledge if it is imparted in his own language. A teacher who cannot convince others should weep on account of his own inability to teach the people in their own language, instead of cursing them and dooming them to live in ignorance and superstition, setting up the plea that the higher knowledge is not for them.
                                                    (CW. 5.263)

Of course, scholarship is an excellent thing; but cannot scholarship be displayed through any other medium than a language that is stiff and unintelligible, that is unnatural and merely artificial? Is there no room for art in the spoken language?   (CW. 6.187)

The language in which we naturally express ourselves, in which we communicate our anger, grief, or love, etc.—there cannot be a fitter language than that. We must stick to that idea, that manner of expression, that diction and all. No artificial language can ever have that force, and that brevity and expressiveness, or admit of being given any turn you please, as that spoken language. Language must be made like pure steel—turn and twist it any way you like; it is again the same—it cleaves a rock in twain at one stroke, without its edge being turned. Our language is becoming artificial by imitating the slow and pompous movement—and only that—of Sanskrit. And language is the chief means and index of a nation's progress.   (CW. 6.187-8)

In our country, owing to all learning being in Sanskrit from the ancient times, there has arisen an immeasurable gulf between the learned and the common folk. All the great personages, from Buddha down to Chaitanya and Ramakrishna, who came for the well-being of the world, taught the common people in the language of the people themselves.
                                                              (CW. 6.187)

What is the use of creating an unnatural language to the exclusion of the natural one? Do you not think out your scholastic researches in the language which you are accustomed to speak at home? Why then do you introduce such a queer and unwieldy thing when you proceed to put them in black and white? The language in which you think out philosophy and science in your mind and argue with others in public—is not that the language for writing philosophy and science?
                                                              (CW. 6.187)

THE SANSKRIT LANGUAGE

My idea is first of all to bring out the gems of spirituality that are stored up in our books and in the possession of a few only, hidden, as it were, in monasteries and forests—to bring them out; to bring the knowledge out of them, not only from the hands where it is hidden, but from the still more inaccessible chest, the language in which it is preserved, the incrustation of centuries of Sanskrit words. In one word, I want to make them popular. I want to bring out these ideas and let them be the common property of all, of every man in India, whether he knows the Sanskrit language or not. ... Therefore the ideas must be taught in the language of the people; at the same time, Sanskrit education must go on along with it, because the very sound of Sanskrit words gives a prestige and a power and a strength to the race. The attempts of the great Rāmānuja and of Chaitanya and of Kabir to raise the lower classes of India show that marvellous results were attained during the lifetime of those great prophets; yet the later failures have to be explained, and cause shown why the effect of their teachings stopped almost within a century of the passing away of these great Masters. The secret is here. They raised the lower classes; they had all the wish that these should come up, but they did not apply their energies to the spreading of the Sanskrit language among the masses.   (CW. 3.290-1)

Even the great Buddha made one false step when he stopped the Sanskrit language from being studied by the masses. He wanted rapid and immediate results, and translated and preached in the language of the day, Pāli. That was grand; he spoke in the language of the people, and the people understood him... It spread the ideas quickly and made them reach far and wide. But along with that, Sanskrit ought to have spread. Knowledge came, but the prestige was not there, culture was not there. ... Until you give them that,... there will be another caste created, having the advantage of the Sanskrit language, which will quickly get above the rest and rule them all the same. (CW. 3.291)

Why do you not become Sanskrit scholars? Why do you not spend millions to bring Sanskrit education to all the castes of India? (CW. 3.298)

Sanskrit is the language of God. (CW. 3.513)

Sanskrit is the divine language. (CW. 3.513)

Sanskrit and prestige go together in India. (CW. 3.299)

One thing that I am very sorry to notice in these parts is the thorough want of Sanskrit and other learning. The people of this part of the country have for their religion a certain bundle of local superstitions about eating, drinking, and bathing, and that is about the whole of their religion. (CW. 8.290)

In philology, our Sanskrit language is now universally acknowledged to be the foundation of all European languages, which, in fact, are nothing but jargonized Sanskrit.
(CW. 2.512)

India has given to antiquity the earliest scientifical physicians, and, according to Sir William Hunter, she has even contributed to modern medical science by the discovery of various chemicals and by teaching you how to reform misshapen ears and noses. Even more it has done in mathematics, for algebra, geometry, astronomy, and the triumph of modern science—mixed mathematics—were all invented in India, just so much as the ten numerals, the very cornerstone of all present civilization, were discovered in India, and are in reality, Sanskrit words. (CW. 2.511)

HIGHER EDUCATION

Our pedagogues are making parrots of our boys and ruining their brains by cramming a lot of subjects into them. ... Goodness gracious! What a fuss and fury about graduating and after a few days all cools down! And after all that, what is it they learn but that what religion and customs we have are all bad, and what the Westerners have are all good! At last, they cannot keep the wolf from the door! What does it matter if this higher education remains or goes?

(CW. 5.366)

Does higher education mean mere study of material sciences and turning out things of everyday use by machinery? The use of higher education is to find out how to solve the problems of life, and this is what is engaging the profound thought of the modern civilized world, but it was solved in our country thousands of years ago. (CW. 5.368)

There is no harm in preaching the idea of elevating the masses by means of a central college, and bringing education as well as religion to the door of the poor by means of missionaries trained in this college. (CW. 5.30)

It is intended to extend the operations of the Math, by educating in the Math as many young men as the funds can afford, in both Western Science and Indian Spirituality, so that in addition to the advantages of a University education, they will acquire a manly discipline by living in contact with their teachers. (CW. 5.435)

The masses in our country are like the sleeping Leviathan. The education imparted by the present university system reaches one or two per cent of the masses only. And even those who get that do not succeed in their endeavours of doing any good to their country. But it is not their fault, poor fellows! As soon as they come out of their college, they find themselves fathers of several children. (CW. 5.380)

Those who are removed one stage higher than these, having read a few pages of English, hang about the thresholds of public offices with petitions in their hands. In the case of a post of twenty or thirty rupees falling vacant, five hundred B.A.s and M.A.s will apply for it! And, dear me! How curiously worded these petitions are! 'I have nothing to eat at home, sir, my wife and children are starving; I most humbly implore you, sir, to give me some means to provide for myself and my family, or we shall die of starvation!" Even when they enter into service, they cast all self-respect to the winds and servitude in its worst form is what they practice. Such is the condition, then, of the masses. The highly-educated, prominent men among you form themselves into societies and clamour at the top of their voices: "Alas! India is going to ruin, day by day!' (CW. 5.354)

We have seen that of books, of education in our sense of the word, he [Sri Ramakrishna] had none, and so much the more natural, so much the more healthy, was his mind, so much the purer his thoughts, undiluted by drinking in the thoughts of others. Because he did not go to the university, therefore he thought for himself. Because we have spent half of our lives in the university we are filled with a collection of other people's thoughts.   (CW. 4.167-8)

The old Sanskrit universities are mainly composed of boys. The girls very rarely go up to those universities; but there are a few exceptions.   (CW. 8.69)

I studied hard for twelve years and became a graduate of Kolkata University; now I can scarcely make $5.00 a month in my country. Would you believe it? It is actually a fact. So these educational institutions of foreigners are simply to get a lot of useful, practical slaves for a little money—to turn out a host of clerks, postmasters, telegraph operators, and so on.
                                                            (CW. 8.69-70)

We must have a college in Madras to teach comparative religions, Sanskrit, the different schools of Vedanta, and some European languages; we must have a press, and papers printed in English and in the Vernaculars. When this is done, then I shall know that you have accomplished something.
                                                            (CW. 5.67)

It would be well to open a Theological College in Madras, and then gradually extend its scope, to give a thorough education to young men in the Vedas and the different Bhāshyas and philosophies, including a knowledge of the other religions of the world. At the same time a paper in English and the vernacular should be started as an organ of the College.
                                                            (CW. 4.371)

Take your universities. What have they done during the fifty years [this was told at Madras in 1897] of their existence?

They have not produced one original man. They are merely an examining body. The idea of the sacrifice for the common weal is not yet developed in our nation.   (CW. 5.224)

Q. What is the defect in the present university system?
A. It is almost wholly one of defects. Why, it is nothing but a perfect machine for turning out clerks. I would even thank my stars if that were all. But no! See how men are becoming destitute of *śraddhā* and faith. They assert that the *Gitā* is only an interpolation, and that the Vedas are but rustic songs! They like to master every detail concerning things and nations outside of India, but if you ask them, they do not know even the names of their own forefathers up to the seventh generation, not to speak of the fourteenth!   (CW. 5.364-5)

There should be an institution to train teachers who must go about preaching religion and giving secular education to our people; they must carry both.   (CW. 3.303)

TECHNICAL EDUCATION

What we need, you know, is to study, independent of foreign control, different branches of the knowledge that is our own, and with it the English language and Western science; we need technical education and all else that may develop industries so that men, instead of seeking for service, may earn enough to provide for themselves, and save something against a rainy day.   (CW. 5.368-9)

If I can get some unmarried graduates, I may try to send them over to Japan and make arrangements for their technical education there, so that when they come back, they may turn their knowledge to the best account for India. What a good thing that would be!   (CW. 5.372)

It would be better if the people got a little technical education, so that they might find work and earn their bread, instead of dawdling about and crying for service.   (CW. 5.367)

PRACTICAL EXPERIENCE

We may talk and reason all our lives, but we shall not understand a word of truth, until we experience it ourselves. You cannot hope to make a man a surgeon by simply giving him a few books. You cannot satisfy my curiosity to see a country by showing me a map; I must have actual experience. Maps can only create curiosity in us to get more perfect knowledge. Beyond that, they have no value whatever.   (CW. 1.185)

We may read books, hear lectures, and talk miles, but experience is the one teacher, the one eye-opener. It is best as it is. We learn, through smiles and tears we learn. (CW. 8.492-3)

Experience is the only teacher we have.   (CW. 1.185)

Practice is absolutely necessary. You may sit down and listen to me by the hour every day, but if you do not practise, you will not get one step further. It all depends on practice. We never understand these things until we experience them. We will have to see and feel them for ourselves. Simply listening to explanations and theories will not do.   (CW. 1.139)

All our knowledge is based upon experience.   (CW. 1.125)

It is practice first, and knowledge afterwards.   (CW. 2.317)

Lectures won't do any good in this country. Our educated countrymen would hear them and, at best, would cheer and clap their hands, saying, 'Well done'; that is all. Then they would go home and digest, as we say, everything they had heard, with their meal! What good will hammering do on a piece of rusty old iron? It will only crumble into pieces. First, it should be made red-hot and then it can be moulded into any shape by hammering. Nothing will avail in our country without setting a glowing and living example before the people.

(CW. 5.352)

I have heard it said that our masses are dense, that they do not want any education, and that they do not care for any information. I had at one time a foolish leaning towards that opinion myself, but I find experience is a far more glorious teacher than any amount of speculation, or any amount of books written by globe-trotters and hasty observers. This experience teaches me that they are not dense, that they are not slow, that they are as eager and thirsty for information as any race under the sun. (CW. 3.147)

You must learn to make the physique very strong and teach the same to others. Don't you find me exercising everyday with dumb-bells even now? Walk in the mornings and evenings and do physical labour. Body and mind must run parallel. It won't do to depend on others in everything. When the necessity of strengthening the physique is brought home to people, they will exert themselves of their own accord. It is to make them feel this need that education is necessary at the present moment. (CW. 7.171-2)

The modern student is not practical. He is quite helpless. What our students want is not so much muscularity of body as hardihood. They are wanting in self-help. They are not accustomed to use their eyes and hands. No handicraft is taught. The present system of English education is entirely literary. The student must be made to think for himself and work for himself. Suppose there is a fire. He is the first to come forward and put out the fire who is accustomed to use his eyes and hands. ... The education that is given is one-sided, weakening, it is killing by inches. The children are made to cram too much of useless matter, and are incarcerated in school rooms fifty or seventy in each, five hours together. ... It is forgotten that the future health of the man is in the child. It is forgotten that nature can never be cheated and things cannot be pushed too early. In giving education to a child the law of growth has to be obeyed. And we must learn to wait. Nothing is more important than that the child must have a strong and healthy body. (CW. 9.546-7)

It will not do merely to listen to great principles. You must apply them in the practical field, turn them into constant practice. (CW. 7.117)

CONCENTRATION

There is only one method by which to attain knowledge, that which is called concentration. (CW. 1.130)

The very essence of education is concentration of mind. (CW. 6.38)

We have but one method of acquiring knowledge. From the lowest man to the highest yogi, all have to use the same method; and that method is what is called concentration. The chemist who works in his laboratory concentrates all the powers of his mind, brings them into one focus, and throws them on the elements; and the elements stand analyzed, and thus his knowledge comes. The astronomer has also concentrated the powers of his mind and brought them into one focus; and he throws them on to objects through his telescope; and stars and systems roll forward and give up their secrets to him. So it is in every case—with the professor in his chair, the student with his book—with every man who is working to know. ... The more this power of concentration, the more knowledge is acquired. (CW. 2.390-1)

The main difference between men and the animals is the difference in their power of concentration. ... An animal has very little power of concentration. Those who have trained animals find much difficulty in the fact that the animal is constantly forgetting what is told him. He cannot concentrate his mind long upon anything at a time. Herein is the difference between man and the animals... The difference in their power of concentration also constitutes the difference between man and man. Compare the lowest with the highest man. The difference is in the degree of concentration.   (CW. 6.37)

All success in any line of work is the result of this. High achievements in art, music, etc., are the results of concentration.

(CW. 6.37)

The power of concentration is the only key to the treasure-house of knowledge. ... In the present state of our body we are so much distracted, and the mind is frittering away its energies upon a hundred sorts of things. As soon as I try to calm my thoughts and concentrate my mind upon any one object of knowledge, thousands of undesired impulses rush into the brain, thousands of thoughts rush into the mind and disturb it. How to check it and bring the mind under control is the whole subject of study in *Rāja-Yoga*.   (CW. 2.391)

The practice of meditation... leads to mental concentration.

(CW. 6.486)

To me the very essence of education is concentration of mind, not the collecting of facts. If I had to do my education over again and had any voice in the matter, I would not study facts at all. I would develop the power of concentration and detachment, and then with a perfect instrument I could collect facts at will. Side by side, in the child, should be developed the power of concentration and detachment.   (CW. 6.38-9)

Education is not filling the mind with a lot of facts. Perfecting the instrument and getting complete mastery of my own mind [is the ideal of education]. If I want to concentrate my mind upon a point, it goes there, and the moment I call, it is free [again]. (CW. 1.510)

Concentration is the essence of all knowledge; nothing can be done without it. Ninety per cent of thought force is wasted by the ordinary human being, and therefore he is constantly committing blunders; the trained man or mind never makes a mistake. (CW. 6.123-4)

The present system of education is all wrong. The mind is crammed with facts before it knows how to think. Control of the mind should be taught first. If I had my education to get over again and had any voice in the matter, I would learn to master my mind first, and then gather facts if I wanted them. It takes people a long time to learn things because they can't concentrate their minds at will. (CW. 8.280)

Power comes to him who observes unbroken *brahmacharya* for a period of twelve years. (CW. 5.358)

Complete continence gives great intellectual and spiritual power. (CW. 7.67)

Controlled desire leads to the highest result. Transform the sexual energy into spiritual energy, but do not emasculate, because that is throwing away the power. The stronger this force, the more can be done with it. Only a powerful current of water can do hydraulic mining. (CW. 7.69)

By the observance of strict *brahmacharya* (continence) all learning can be mastered in a very short time—one has an unfailing memory of what one hears or knows but once. It

7

is owing to this want of continence that everything is on the brink of ruin in our country. (CW. 7.224)

The chaste brain has tremendous energy and gigantic will-power. Without chastity there can be no spiritual strength. Continence gives wonderful control over mankind. The spiritual leaders of men have been very continent, and this is what gave them power. (CW. 1.263)

Chastity in thought, word, and deed, always, and in all conditions, is what is called *brahmacharya*. (CW. 1.190)

Unchaste imagination is as bad as unchaste action.
(CW. 7.69)

Every boy should be trained to practise absolute *brahmacharya*, and then, and then only, faith—*śraddhā*—will come.
(CW. 5.369)

The *brahmachārin* must be sexually pure in thought, word, and deed. (CW. 7.67)

No one could obtain intellectual greatness until he was physically pure. Morality gave strength; the immoral were always weak, and could never raise themselves intellectually, much less spiritually. Directly [as] immorality began to enter the national life its foundations commenced to rot. As the life blood of every nation was to be found in the schools, where boys and girls were receiving their education, it was absolutely essential that the young students should be pure, and this purity must be taught them. (CW. 9.519)

The yogis claim that of all the energies that are in the human body the highest is what they call '*ojas*'. Now this *ojas* is stored up in the brain, and the more *ojas* is in a man's head, the more powerful he is, the more intellectual, the more spiritually strong. One man may speak beautiful language and beautiful thoughts, but they do not impress people; another man speaks neither beautiful language nor beautiful thoughts, yet his words charm. Every movement of his is powerful. That is the power of *ojas*.

Now in every man there is more or less of this *ojas* stored up. All the forces that are working in the body in their highest become *ojas*. You must remember that it is only a question of transformation. ... The yogis say that that part of the human energy which is expressed as sex energy, in sexual thought, when checked and controlled, easily becomes changed into *ojas*, ... He tries to take up all his sexual energy and convert it into *ojas*. It is only the chaste man or woman who can make the *ojas* rise and store it in the brain; that is why chastity has always been considered the highest virtue. A man feels that if he is unchaste, spirituality goes away, he loses mental vigour and moral stamina. (CW. 1.169-70)

THE MIND

All these senses, external and internal, must be under the disciple's control. By hard practice he has to arrive at the stage where he can assert his mind against the senses, against the commands of nature. He should be able to say to his mind, 'You are mine; I order you, do not see or hear anything'. ... Next, the mind must be made to quiet down. It is rushing about. Just as I sit down to meditate, all the vilest subjects in the world come up. The whole thing is nauseating. Why should the mind think thoughts I do not want it to think? I am as it were a slave to the mind. (CW. 8.109-10)

The disciple must have great power of endurance. Life seems comfortable; and you find the mind behaves well when everything is going well with you. But if something goes wrong, your mind loses its balance. That is not good. Bear all evil and misery without one murmur of hurt, without one thought of unhappiness, resistance, remedy or retaliation. That is true endurance. (CW. 8.110)

All knowledge that the world has ever received comes from the mind; the infinite library of the universe is in your own mind. The external world is simply the suggestion, the occasion, which sets you to study your own mind, but the object of your study is always your own mind. The falling of an apple gave the suggestion to Newton, and he studied his own mind. He rearranged all the previous links of thought in his mind and discovered a new link among them, which we call the law of gravitation. It was not in the apple nor in anything in the centre of the earth.   (CW. 1.28)

Never allow weakness to overtake your mind.   (CW. 7.234)

Physical weakness is the cause of at least one-third of our miseries. We are lazy, we cannot work; we cannot combine ... we speak of many things parrot-like but never do them; speaking and not doing has become a habit with us. What is the cause of that? Physical weakness. This sort of weak brain is not able to do anything; we must strengthen it.   (CW. 3.241-2)

You have to build the body by good nutritious food—then only will the mind be strong. The mind is but the subtle part of the body. You must retain great strength in your mind and words. 'I am low, I am low'—repeating these ideas in the mind, man belittles and degrades himself. ... He alone who is always awake to the idea of freedom, becomes free; he who thinks he is bound, endures life after life in the state of bondage. ... Be a hero. Always say, 'I have no fear'. ... Fear is death, fear is sin, fear is hell, fear is unrighteousness, fear is wrong life. All the negative thoughts and ideas that are in this world have proceeded from this evil spirit of fear. ... Therefore I say, 'Be fearless, be fearless'.   (CW. 7.135-6)

All knowledge depends upon calmness of mind.   (CW. 7.72)

If you have to think, think good thoughts, great thoughts.
                                                (CW. 8.131)

It is our own mental attitude which makes the world what it is for us. Our thoughts make things beautiful, our thoughts make things ugly. The whole world is in our minds. Learn to see things in the proper light. (CW. 1.441)

Doing is very good, but that comes from thinking. ... Fill the brain, therefore, with high thoughts, highest ideals, place them day and night before you, and out of that will come great work. (CW. 2.86)

We are what our thoughts have made us; so take care of what you think. (CW. 7.14)

What we think we become. (CW. 8.19)

Like fire in a piece of flint, knowledge exists in the mind; suggestion is the friction which brings it out. (CW. 1.28)

All knowledge, therefore, secular or spiritual, is in the human mind. In many cases it is not discovered, but remains covered, and when the covering is being slowly taken off, we say, 'We are learning,' and the advance of knowledge is made by the advance of this process of uncovering. The man from whom this veil is being lifted is the more knowing man, the man upon whom it lies thick is ignorant, and the man from whom it has entirely gone is all-knowing, omniscient. (CW. 1.28)

Books suggest the inner light and the method of bringing that out, but we can only understand them when we have earned the knowledge ourselves. When the inner light has flashed for you, let the books go, and look only within. You have in you all and a thousand times more than is in all the books. Never lose faith in yourself, you can do anything in this universe. Never weaken, all power is yours. (CW. 7.85)

POWER OF KNOWLEDGE

Pleasure is not the goal of man, but knowledge. (CW. 1.27)

Knowledge is the goal of all life. (CW. 4.210)

The real life of man consists of knowledge. (CW. 1.52)

Instinct, reason, and inspiration are the three instruments of knowledge. (CW. 2.389)

The gift of knowledge is the highest gift in the world. (CW. 7.256)

No action can give you freedom; only knowledge can make you free. (CW. 7.54)

Knowledge is irresistible; the mind cannot take it or reject it. When it comes the mind has to accept it; so it is not a work of the mind; only, its expression comes in the mind. (CW. 7.54)

Knowledge itself is the highest reward of knowledge. (CW. 1.130)

Knowledge alone can make us perfect. (CW. 7.38)

From my childhood everyone around me taught weakness; I have been told ever since I was born that I was a weak thing. It is very difficult for me now to realize my own strength, but by analysis and reasoning I gain knowledge of my own strength, I realise it. All the knowledge that we have in this world, where did it come from? It was within us. What knowledge is outside? None. Knowledge was not in matter; it was in man all the time. Nobody ever created knowledge; man brings it from within. (CW. 2.339)

MUSIC AND ART

In music, India gave to the world her system of notation, with the seven cardinal notes and the diatonic scale, all of which we enjoyed as early as 350 B.C., while it came to Europe only in the eleventh century. (CW. 2.511-2)

Music in which the notes follow each other in rapid succession holds the mind readily. A child loves lively music, because the rapidity of the notes gives the mind no chance to wander. (CW. 6.37)

When we hear beautiful music, our minds become fastened upon it. (CW. 6.37)

There is science in *Dhrupad*, *Kheyal*, etc., but it is in *Kirtana*, i.e. *Māthura* and *Viraha* and other like compositions that there is real music—for there is feeling. Feeling is the soul, the secret of everything. There is more music in common people's songs, and they should be collected together. The science of *Dhrupad* etc., applied to the music of *Kirtana* will produce the perfect music. (CW. 7.407)

In literature, our epics and poems and dramas rank as high as those of any language; our '*Shaguntala*' [Shakuntala] was summarized by Germany's greatest poet, as 'heaven and earth united'. India has given to the world the fables of Aesop, which were copied by Aesop from an old Sanskrit book; it has given the *Arabian Nights*, yes, even the story of Cinderella and the Bean Stalks.   (CW. 2.512)

In art, interest must be centred on the principal theme. Drama is the most difficult of all arts. In it two things are to be satisfied—first, the ears, and second, the eyes. To paint a scene, if one thing be painted, it is easy enough; but to paint different things and yet to keep up the central interest is very difficult. Another difficult thing is stage-management, that is, combining different things in such a manner as to keep the central interest intact.   (CW. 7.407)

True art can be compared to a lily which springs from the ground, takes its nourishment from the ground, is in touch with the ground, and yet is quite high above it. So art must be in touch with nature—and wherever that touch is gone, art degenerates—yet it must be above nature.   (CW. 5.258)

Art is—representing the beautiful. There must be art in everything. The difference between architecture and building is that the former expresses an idea, while the latter is merely a structure built on economical principles. The value of matter depends solely on its capacities of expressing ideas.

(CW. 5.259)

In India, music was developed to the full seven notes, even to half and quarter notes, ages ago. India led in music, also in drama and sculpture. Whatever is done now is merely an attempt at imitation.   (CW. 4.196-7)

Now will people gradually understand that a language, or art, or music that expresses no meaning and is lifeless, is of no good. Now they will understand that the more strength is infused into the national life, the more will language, art, and music, etc. become spontaneously instinct with ideas and life. (CW. 6.189)

Glancing at a highly finished painting we cannot understand where its beauty lies. Moreover, unless the eye is, to a certain extent, trained, one cannot appreciate the subtle touches and blendings, the inner genius of a work of art. In painting, by keeping in touch with nature, you can make it as artistic as you like; there is no harm in doing that, and the result will be nothing but good. Similarly, in music, you can display any amount of skill by keeping to science, and it will be pleasing to the ear. Unless each note is given full play in every scale, all the science of music is marred. (CW. 5.361-2)

When one note comes upon another in quick succession, it not only robs music of all grace, but, on the other hand, creates discordance rather. Again, the poetry of music is completely destroyed if there be in it such profuse use of light and short strains just for effect. To sing by keeping to the idea, meant to be conveyed by a song, totally disappeared from our country. Nowadays, it seems, the true art is reviving a little with the improvement in theatres; but, on the other hand, all regard for *rāgas* and *rāginis* is being more and more flung to the winds. (CW. 5.362-3)

CHARACTER-BUILDING

It is nowadays a common practice in our society, to signify virtues or morals as values. This practice is born of a reluctance to use the terms morals and virtues since they carry a religious connotation. But Swami Vivekananda had no such qualms and he does not use the terms values or value education.

Avoiding pedagogic terms, he used words familiar to the common man. He gave a clarion call to cultivate the highest moral and spiritual virtues like faith in one's divine nature (called Atman or Soul or Spirit in different traditions), truth, purity, honesty, perseverance, courage, strength, love, sympathy for and service to all, modesty, humility, and politeness.

The Swami strongly felt that religion should form the core of education. By religion he meant not some sectarian or dogmatic beliefs, but spirituality—the kernel or common essence of all denominational religions. Such education he said, would help an individual to develop a perfect character. Many of his thoughts on cultivating virtues have been compiled in the following two chapters.

1. Character: Its Importance and Making

If you really want to judge of the character of a man, look not at his great performances. Every fool may become a hero at one time or another. Watch a man do his most common actions; those are indeed the things which will tell you the real character of a great man. Great occasions rouse even the lowest of human beings to some kind of greatness, but he alone is the really great man whose character is great always, the same wherever he be. (CW. 1.29)

Men, men, these are wanted: everything else will be ready, but strong, vigorous, believing young men, sincere to the backbone, are wanted. A hundred such and the world becomes revolutionized. (CW. 3.223-4)

Money does not pay, nor name; fame does not pay, nor learning. It is love that pays; it is character that cleaves its way through adamantine walls of difficulties. (CW. 4.367)

Be moral. Be brave. Be a heart-whole man. Strictly moral, brave unto desperation. Don't bother your head with religious theories. Cowards only sin, brave men never, no, not even in mind. Try to love anybody and everybody ... No religion for you, my children, but morality and bravery. No cowardice, no sin, no crime, no weakness—the rest will come of itself. (CW. 5.3)

Nothing else is necessary but these—love, sincerity, and patience. (CW. 4.367)

The road to the Good is the roughest and steepest in the universe. It is a wonder that so many succeed, no wonder that so many fall. Character has to be established through a thousand stumbles. (CW. 8.383)

Therefore, stand up, be bold, be strong. Take the whole responsibility on your own shoulders, and know that you are the creator of your own destiny. (CW. 2.225)

The miseries of the world cannot be cured by physical help only. Until man's nature changes, these physical needs will always arise, and miseries will always be felt, and no amount of physical help will cure them completely. The only solution of this problem is to make mankind pure. Ignorance is the mother of all the evil and all the misery we see. Let men have light, let them be pure and spiritually strong and educated, then alone will misery cease in the world, not before. We may convert every house in the country into a charity asylum, we may fill the land with hospitals, but the misery of man will still continue to exist until man's character changes.

(CW. 1.53)

Who will give the world light? Sacrifice in the past has been the law, it will be, alas, for ages to come. The earth's bravest and best will have to sacrifice themselves for the good of many, for the welfare of all. Buddhas by the hundred are necessary with eternal love and pity.   (CW. 7.501)

Love never fails, my son; today or tomorrow or ages after, truth will conquer. Love shall win the victory. Do you love your fellow men?... If so, you are irresistible. It is character that pays everywhere.   (CW. 5.51)

Your country requires heroes; be heroes!   (CW. 5.51)

The character of any man, it really is but the aggregate of tendencies, the sum total of the bent of his mind. As pleasure and pain pass before his soul, they leave upon it different pictures, and the result of these combined impressions is what is called a man's character.   (CW. 1.27)

Every work that we do, every movement of the body, every thought that we think, leaves such impressions on the mind-stuff, and even when such impressions are not obvious on the surface, they are sufficiently strong to work beneath the surface, subconsciously. ... Each man's character is determined by the sum total of these impressions. If good impressions prevail, the character becomes good, if bad, it becomes bad.

(CW. 1.54)

You must have strict morality. Deviate an inch from this, and you are gone for ever. (CW. 7.447)

It is said, 'Habit is second nature', it is first nature also, and the whole nature of man; everything that we are is the result of habit. That gives us consolation, because, if it is only habit, we can make and unmake it at any time. ... The only remedy for bad habits is counter habits; all the bad habits that have left their impressions are to be controlled by good habits. Go on doing good, thinking holy thoughts continuously; that is the only way to suppress base impressions. Never say any man is hopeless, because he only represents a character, a bundle of habits, which can be checked by new and better ones. Character is repeated habits, and repeated habits alone can reform character. (CW. 1.207-8)

2. Some Principal Virtues of Character

A. FAITH IN ONE'S DIVINE SELF
B. TRUTH, UNSELfISHNESS, LOVE, AND SERVICE
C. STRENGTH
D. PATRIOTISM

A. FAITH IN ONE'S DIVINE SELF

Faith, faith, faith in ourselves, faith, faith in God—this is the secret of greatness. (CW. 3.190)

All power is within you; you can do anything and everything. Believe in that, do not believe that you are weak. ... All power is there. Stand up and express the divinity within you.

(CW. 3.284)

Ye are the children of God, the sharers of immortal bliss, holy and perfect beings. Ye divinities on earth—sinners! It is a sin to call a man so. (CW. 1.11)

Do you know how much energy, how many powers, how many forces are still lurking behind that frame of yours? What scientist has known all that is in man? Millions of years have passed since man first came here, and yet but one infinitesimal part of his powers has been manifested. Therefore, you must not say that you are weak. How do you know what possibilities lie behind that degradation on the surface? You know but little of that which is within you. For behind you is the ocean of infinite power and blessedness. (CW. 2.301-2)

The history of the world is the history of a few men who had faith in themselves. That faith calls out the divinity within. You can do anything. You fail only when you do not strive sufficiently to manifest infinite power. As soon as a man or a nation loses faith, death comes. (CW. 8.228)

Teach yourselves, teach every one his real nature, call upon the sleeping soul and see how it awakes. Power will come, glory will come, goodness will come, purity will come, and everything that is excellent will come when this sleeping soul is roused to self-conscious activity. (CW. 3.193)

If the fisherman thinks that he is the Spirit, he will be a better fisherman; if the student thinks he is the Spirit, he will be a better student. If the lawyer thinks that he is the Spirit, he will be a better lawyer. (CW. 3.245)

All beings, great or small, are equally manifestations of God; the difference is only in the manifestation. (CW. 1.424)

This *śraddhā* is what I want, and what all of us here want, this faith in ourselves, and before you is the great task to get that faith. Give up the awful disease that is creeping into our national blood, that idea of ridiculing everything, that loss of seriousness. Give that up. Be strong and have this *śraddhā*, and everything else is bound to follow. (CW. 3.320)

Man is to become divine by realizing the divine. (CW. 1.16)

The ideal of faith in ourselves is of the greatest help to us. If faith in ourselves had been more extensively taught and practiced, I am sure a very large portion of the evils and miseries that we have would have vanished. (CW. 2.301)

B. TRUTH, UNSELfiSHNESS, LOVE, AND SERVICE

Truth can be stated in a thousand different ways, yet each one can be true. (CW. 5.410)

Truth is purity, truth is all-knowledge; truth must be strengthening, must be enlightening, must be invigorating.
(CW. 3.225)

Truth does not pay homage to any society, ancient or modern. Society has to pay homage to truth or die. Societies should be moulded upon truth, and truth has not to adjust itself to society. (CW. 2.84)

8

That society is the greatest, where the highest truths become practical. That is my opinion; and if society is not fit for the highest truths, make it so; and the sooner, the better.

(CW. 2.85)

Practise that boldness which dares know the Truth, which dares show the Truth in life. (CW. 2.85)

Truth, purity, and unselfishness—wherever these are present, there is no power below or above the sun to crush the possessor thereof. Equipped with these, one individual is able to face the whole universe in opposition. (CW. 4.279)

Everything can be sacrificed for truth, but truth cannot be sacrificed for anything. (CW 5.410)

Unselfishness is God. (CW. 1.87)

Unselfishness is more paying, only people have not the patience to practise it. (CW. 1.32)

Man thinks foolishly that he can make himself happy, and after years of struggle finds out at last that true happiness consists in killing selfishness and that no one can make him happy except himself. (CW. 1.84)

The only definition that can be given of morality is this: That which is selfish is immoral, and that which is unselfish is moral. (CW. 1.110)

This unselfishness is the test of religion. He who has more of this unselfishness is more spiritual and nearer to Śiva.

(CW. 3.143)

Do not stand on a high pedestal and take five cents in your hand and say, 'Here, my poor man,' but be grateful that the poor man is there, so that by making a gift to him you are able to help yourself. It is not the receiver that is blessed, but it is the giver. Be thankful that you are allowed to exercise your power of benevolence and mercy in the world, and thus become pure and perfect. (CW. 1.76)

He who sees Śiva in the poor, in the weak, and in the diseased, really worships Śiva; and if he sees Śiva only in the image, his worship is but preliminary. He who has served and helped one poor man seeing Śiva in him, without thinking of his caste, or creed, or race, or anything, with him Śiva is more pleased than with the man who sees Him only in temples. (CW. 3.142)

Loving others is virtue; hating others is sin. (CW. 5.419)

Where should you go to seek for God—are not all the poor, the miserable, the weak, Gods? Why not worship them first?
(CW. 5.51)

C. STRENGTH

This is the great fact: strength is life, weakness is death. Strength is felicity, life eternal, immortal; weakness is constant strain and misery: weakness is death. (CW. 2.3)

The remedy for weakness is not brooding over weakness, but thinking of strength. Teach men of the strength that is already within them. (CW. 2.300)

Strength and manliness are virtue; weakness and cowardice are sin. Independence is virtue; dependence is sin. Loving others is virtue; hating others is sin. Faith in God and in one's own Self is virtue; doubt is sin. (CW. 5.419)

Only cowards and those who are weak commit sin and tell lies. The brave are always moral. Try to be moral, try to be brave, try to be sympathizing. (CW. 5.3)

This is the only sin—to say that you are weak, or others are weak. (CW. 2.308)

Infinite strength is religion and God. Avoid weakness and slavery. (CW. 7.13)

D. PATRIOTISM

Whether you believe in spirituality or not, for the sake of the national life, you have to get a hold on spirituality and keep to it. Then stretch the other hand out and gain all you can from other races, but everything must be subordinated to that one ideal of life; and out of that a wonderful, glorious, future India will come—I am sure it is coming—a greater India than ever was. (CW. 3.153-4)

If there is any land on this earth. ... where humanity has attained its highest towards gentleness, towards generosity, towards purity, towards calmness, above all, the land of introspection and of spirituality—it is India. (CW. 3.105)

Here in this blessed land, the foundation, the backbone, the life-centre is religion and religion alone. (CW. 3.148)

In India, religious life forms the centre, the keynote of the whole music of national life. (CW. 3.220)

Our sacred motherland is a land of religion and philosophy—the birthplace of spiritual giants—the land of renunciation, where and where alone, from the most ancient to the most modern times, there has been the highest ideal of life open to man. (CW. 3.137)

Have you got the will to surmount mountain-high obstructions? If the whole world stands against you sword in hand, would you still dare to do what you think is right? ... Have you got that steadfastness? If you have these three things, each one of you will work miracles.

(CW. 3.226-7)

I believe in patriotism, and I also have my own ideal of patriotism. Three things are necessary. ... First, feel from the heart. ... Feel, therefore, my would-be reformers, my would-be patriots! Do you feel? Do you feel that millions and millions of the descendants of gods and of sages have become next-door neighbours to brutes? Do you feel that millions are starving today, and millions have been starving for ages? Do you feel that ignorance has come over the land as a dark cloud? Does it make you restless? Does it make you sleepless? Has it gone into your blood, coursing through your veins, becoming consonant with your heartbeats? Has it made you almost mad? Are you seized with that one idea of the misery of ruin, and have you forgotten all about your name, your fame, your wives, your children, your property, even your own bodies? Have you done that? That is the first step to become a patriot, the very first step. (CW. 3.225-6)

You may feel, then; but instead of spending your energies in frothy talk, have you found any way out, any practical solution, some help instead of condemnation, some sweet words to soothe their miseries, to bring them out of this living death? (CW. 3.226)

O India! Forget not... forget not that the lower classes, the ignorant, the poor, the illiterate, the cobbler, the sweeper, are thy flesh and blood, thy brothers. (CW. 4.479-80)

When you have men who are ready to sacrifice their everything for their country, sincere to the backbone—when such men arise, India will become great in every respect. It is the men that make the country! (CW. 5.210)

Let us all work hard, my brethren; this is no time for sleep. On our work depends the coming of the India of the future. She is there ready waiting. She is only sleeping. Arise and awake and see her seated here on her eternal throne, rejuvenated, more glorious than she ever was—this motherland of ours.
(CW. 3.154)

None can resist her any more; never is she going to sleep any more; no outward powers can hold her back any more; for the infinite giant is rising to her feet. (CW. 3.146)

HARMONY OF RELIGIONS

1. THE ESSENCE OF RELIGION

I look upon religion as the innermost core of education. Mind, I do not mean my own, or any one else's opinion about religion. I think the teacher should take the pupils' starting-point in this ... and enable them to develop along their own line of least resistance. (CW. 5.231)

Religion is not in books, nor in theories, nor in dogmas, nor in talking, not even in reasoning. It is being and becoming. (CW. 3.253)

I do not believe in a God or religion which cannot wipe the widow's tears or bring a piece of bread to the orphan's mouth. (CW. 5.50)

The true eternal principles have to be held before the people. ... First of all, we have to introduce the worship of the great saints. Those great-souled ones who have realised the eternal truths are to be presented before the people as the ideals to be followed;—Sri Rāmachandra, Sri Krishna, Mahāvira, and Sri Ramakrishna among others. (CW. 5.387-8)

Religion is the manifestation of the divinity already in man. (CW. 4.358)

Religion is the manifestation of the natural strength that is in man. (CW. 8.185)

Realization is real religion, all the rest is only preparation.

(CW. 1.232)

The old religions said that he was an atheist who did not believe in God. The new religion says that he is the atheist who does not believe in himself. It means faith in all, because you are all. ... It is the great faith which will make the world better. (CW.2.301)

Every religion and every creed recognizes man as divine.

(CW. 8.199)

Each soul is potentially divine. The goal is to manifest this divinity within, by controlling nature, external and internal. Do this either by work, or worship, or psychic control, or philosophy—by one or more or all of these—and be free. This is the whole of religion. Doctrines, or dogmas, or rituals, or books, or temples, or forms, are but secondary details.

(CW. 1.257)

Confucius, Moses, and Pythagoras; Buddha, Christ, Mohammed; Luther, Calvin, and the Sikhs; Theosophy, Spiritualism, and the like; all these mean only the preaching of the Divine-in-man. (CW. 8.229)

There are three things in the make-up of man. There is the body, there is the mind, and there is the soul.

(CW. 5.463-64)

After so much austerity, I have understood this as the real truth—God is present in every *jiva* [individual soul]; there is no other God besides that. 'Who serves *jiva*, serves God indeed'. (CW. 7.247)

By the study of different religions we find that in essence they are one. ... There are differences in non-essentials, but in essentials they are all one. (CW. 1. 317-8)

In the first place, all religions admit that, apart from the body which perishes, there is a certain part or something which does not change like the body, a part that is immutable, eternal, that never dies. (CW. 1.318)

Along with this idea of the soul we find another group of ideas in regard to its perfection. (CW. 1.319)

We find that all religions teach the eternity of the soul, as well as that its lustre has been dimmed, and that its primitive purity is to be regained by the knowledge of God.
(CW. 1.322)

Temples or churches, books or forms, are simply the kindergarten of religion, to make the spiritual child strong enough to take higher steps. ... Religion is not in doctrines, in dogmas, nor in intellectual argumentation; it is being and becoming, it is realization. (CW. 2.43)

Religions of the world have become lifeless mockeries. What the world wants is character. The world is in need of those whose life is one burning love, selfless. That love will make every word tell like thunderbolt. (CW. 7.501)

Now comes the question: Can religion really accomplish anything? It can. It brings to man eternal life. It has made man what he is, and will make of this human animal a god. That is what religion can do. Take religion from human society and what will remain? Nothing but a forest of brutes. (CW. 3.4)

Religion is the idea which is raising the brute unto man, and man unto God. (CW. 5.409)

My children, the secret of religion lies not in theories but in practice. To be good and to do good—that is the whole of religion. (CW. 6.245)

2. HARMONY OF RELIGIONS

All religions are true. (CW. 6.117)

I learnt from my Master [Sri Ramakrishna] ... the wonderful truth that the religions of the world are not contradictory or antagonistic. They are but various phases of one eternal religion. (CW. 4.180)

Sri Ramakrishna never spoke a harsh word against anyone. So beautifully tolerant was he that every sect thought that he belonged to them. He loved every one. To him all religions were true. (CW. 7.24)

His [Sri Ramakrishna's] whole life was spent in breaking down the barriers of sectarianism and dogma. (CW. 5.186)

Our watchword, then, will be acceptance, and not exclusion. ... I accept all religions that were in the past, and worship with them all; I worship God with every one of them, in whatever form they worship Him. I shall go to the mosque of the Mohammedan; I shall enter the Christian's church and kneel before the crucifix; I shall enter the Buddhistic temple, where I shall take refuge in Buddha and in his Law. I shall go into the forest and sit down in meditation with the Hindu, who is trying to see the Light which enlightens the heart of every one.

Not only shall I do all these, but I shall keep my heart open for all that may come in the future. Is God's book finished? Or is it still a continuous revelation going on? It is a marvellous book—these spiritual revelations of the world. The Bible, the Vedas, the Koran, and all other sacred books are but so many pages, and an infinite number of pages remain yet to be unfolded. ... We take in all that has been in the past, enjoy the light of the present, and open every window of the heart for all that will come in the future. Salutation to all the prophets of the past, to all the great ones of the present, and to all that are to come in the future!   (CW. 2.374)

If the Parliament of Religions has shown anything to the world it is this: It has proved to the world that holiness, purity and charity are not the exclusive possessions of any church in the world, and that every system has produced men and women of the most exalted character. In the face of this evidence, if anybody dreams of the exclusive survival of his own religion and the destruction of the others, I pity him from the bottom of my heart, and point out to him that upon the banner of every religion will soon be written, in spite of resistance: 'Help and not Fight,' 'Assimilation and not Destruction,' 'Harmony and Peace and not Dissension.'

(CW. 1.24)

I do not deprecate the existence of sects in the world. Would to God there were twenty millions more, for the more there are, there will be a greater field for selection. What I do object to is trying to fit one religion to every case. Though all religions are essentially the same, they must have the varieties of form produced by dissimilar circumstances among different nations. We must each have our own individual religion, individual so far as the externals of it go.   (CW. 1.325-6)

Swami Vivekananda in California, 1900

SWAMI VIVEKANANDA
AS SEEN BY WORLD THINKERS

Rooted in the past and full of pride in India's prestige, Vivekananda was yet modern in his approach to life's problems and was a kind of bridge between the past of India and her present. ... He was a fine figure of a man, imposing, full of poise and dignity, sure of himself and his mission, and at the same time full of a dynamic and fiery energy and a passion to push India forward.

—Jawaharlal Nehru

Vivekananda was a soul of puissance, if ever there was one, a very lion among men, but the definite work he has left behind is quite incommensurate with our impression of his creative might and energy. We perceive his influence still working gigantically, we know not well how, we know not well where, in something that is not yet formed, something leonine, grand, intuitive, upheaving, that has entered the soul of India, and we say, 'Behold, Vivekananda still lives in the soul of his Mother, and in the souls of her children.'

—Sri Aurobindo

I cannot write about Vivekananda without going into raptures. Few, indeed, could comprehend or fathom him—even amongst those who had the privilege of becoming intimate with him. His personality was rich, profound, and complex, and it was this personality—as distinct from his teachings and writings—which accounts for the wonderful influence he has exerted on his countrymen. ... Reckless in his sacrifice, unceasing in his activity, boundless in his love, profound and versatile in his wisdom, exuberant in his emotions, merciless in his attacks, but yet simple as a child—he was a rare personality in this world of ours.

It is very difficult to explain the versatile genius of Swami Vivekananda. The impact Swami Vivekananda made on students of our times by his works and speeches far outweighed that made by any other leader of the country. He, as it were, expressed fully their hopes and aspirations.

—*Subhas Chandra Bose*

Vivekananda not only made us conscious of our strength, he also pointed out our defects and drawbacks. ... Speaking of those who enjoyed the luxury of studying philosophy and the scriptures in the smugness of their retired life, he said football-playing was better than that type of indulgence. Swamiji made us see the truth that *tattva-jnāna*, which had no place in our everyday relationship with our fellow beings, and in our activities was useless and inane.

—*Vinoba Bhave*

His pre-eminent characteristic was kingliness. He was a born king, and nobody ever came near him either in India or America without paying homage to his majesty. ...His strength and beauty, the grace and dignity of his bearing, the dark light of his eyes, his imposing appearance, and from the moment he began to speak, the splendid music of his rich deep voice enthralled the vast audience of American Anglo-Saxons, previously prejudiced against him on account of his colour. The thought of this warrior prophet of India left a deep mark upon the United States.

It was impossible to imagine him in the second place. Wherever he went he was the first. ... Everybody recognized in him at sight the leader, the anointed of God, the man marked with the stamp of the power to command.

...His words are great music, phrases in the style of Beethoven, stirring rhythms like the march of Handel choruses. I cannot touch these sayings of his, scattered as they are through the pages of books at thirty years' distance, without receiving a thrill through my body like an electric shock. And what shocks, what transports must have been produced when in burning words they issued from the lips of the hero!

—*Romain Rolland*

Reading and re-reading the works of Vivekananda each time I find in them something new that helps deeper to understand India, its philosophy, the way of life and customs of the people in the past and the present, their dreams of the future. ... I think that Vivekananda's greatest service is the development in his teaching of the lofty ideals of humanism which incorporate the finest features of Indian culture. ... Many years will pass, many generations will come and go, Vivekananda and his time will become the distant past, but never will there fade the memory of the man who all his life dreamed of a better future for his people, who did so much to awaken his compatriots and move India forward.

—*E. P. Chelishev*

Even now a hundred years after the birth of Narendranath Datta, who later became Swami Vivekananda, it is very difficult to evaluate his importance in the scale of world history. It is certainly far greater than any Western historian or most Indian historians would have suggested at the time of his death. The passing of the years and the many stupendous and unexpected events which have occurred since then suggests that in centuries to come he will be remembered as one of the main moulders of the modern world, especially as far as Asia is concerned, and as one of the most significant figures in the whole history of Indian religion, comparable in importance to such great teachers as Śankara and Rāmānuja, and definitely more important than the saints of local or regional significance such as Kabir, Chaitanya, and the many Nāyanmārs and Ālwars of South India.

—*A. L. Basham*

A striking figure, clad in yellow and orange, shining like the sun of India in the midst of the heavy atmosphere of Chicago, a lion head, piercing eyes, mobile lips, movements swift and fast—such was my first impression of Swami Vivekananda, as I met him in one of the rooms set apart for the use of the delegates to the Parliament of Religions. Monk, they called him, not unwarrantably, but warrior-monk was he, and the first impression was of the warrior rather than of the monk, for he was off the platform, and his figure was instinct with pride of country, pride of race—the representative of the oldest of living religions, surrounded by curious gazers of nearly the youngest, and by no means inclined to give step, as though the hoary faith he embodied was in aught inferior to the noblest there. ...Enraptured, the huge multitude hung upon his words; not a syllable must be lost, not a cadence missed! 'That man a heathen!' said one, as he came out of the great hall, 'and we send missionaries to his people! It would be more fitting that they should send missionaries to us.'

—*Annie Besant*